Praise for Seven Days To Sexy

"For years Dr. Anna has been our family's go-to for all of our skin care concerns. She keeps us looking good and feeling great! And as we like to say, you never have to get ready if you are already ready."

—Rebecca Romijn, actress, model

"Dr. Anna has been my dermatologist in Calabasas for the past five years. She's the best ever!"

— Olivia Culpo model, actress, Miss Universe

"This is the beauty bible! Dr. Anna is a perfectionist who knows the secrets for perfecting skin. In her book, Seven Days to Sexy, she explores the science behind beauty and also provides real world tips that women can use in order to look and feel their absolute best!"

— Alyssa Milano, actress

"I've been seeing Dr Guanche for years now. Looking great is part of my job description. She keeps me looking and feeling my best! Dr Guanche is innovative and artistic. I call her the Steve Jobs of Dermatology!"

— Eva LaRue, actress, model

"Dr. Anna Guanche is every A-lister's best kept secret weapon, to help keep them looking and feeling their absolute best!"

— Susan Holmes McKagan, supermodel,
bestselling author of *The Velvet Rose*

"Dr. Guanche makes me feel great about my skin. Every product she recommends is like magic in a bottle. When I come in to see her I feel I can trust her to be honest and keep me looking natural."

— Meegan Hodges, rock music photographer, public figure

"Dr. Anna Guanche is a respected member of the Cosmetic Dermatology community. After years of preparing supermodels and actresses for the red carpet, I trust she has the insider beauty secrets that take a person's look to the next level!"

— Doris Day, MD, Professor of Dermatology,
NYU Langone Medical Center,
and Author of *Forget the Facelift*
and *100 Questions and Answers about Acne*

Seven Days to Sexy

Insider secrets from a celebrity beauty doctor

Publisher:
Bella Skin Institute
23622 Calabasas Rd Suite 339
Calabasas, CA 91302

Photographs courtesy of Troy Jenson

Printed in the United States of America

Seven Days To Sexy - Insider secrets from a celebrity beauty doctor
Anna D. Guanche, MD

1. Title 2. Author 3. Beauty, Self-Help

Library of Congress Control Number: 2019909360
ISBN 13: 978-0-578-50183-3

Seven Days to Sexy

Insider secrets from a celebrity beauty doctor

ANNA D. GUANCHE, MD

Bella Skin Institute

This book is dedicated to

My Patients, the Bella Skin Institute Derm Dream Team

and My Family: Carlos, Bella and Carlos

Contents

Introduction

It only takes *seven* days to get sexy? That is the first question that blurts out of people's mouths when I introduce this book. Yes! The truth is, you are already sexy. Sex is how you got here, and it is a deeply ingrained trait that we all share. Of course, we each have our own spin on it—thank goodness! One could argue that seven minutes is all it takes to bring out the sexy...but what we are discussing here are proven beauty tips and procedures that allow us to unleash our sexiest self within seven days. This book incorporates what we have learned from human sexuality research, what we see in pop culture, and what I've learned from some of our sexiest icons that I know to point us in the right direction. Then it provides you with information and accessible products and procedures to help you realize a seven-day, seven-week, seven-month plan to become your absolute best.

What do you envision when you hear the word "sexy?" For some, the image of a particular supermodel, actress, or celebrity may come to mind. For others, sexy may suggest a certain attire, look, or demeanor. You might even link sexy to one person who epitomizes the word. Words associated with sexy typically include sultry, seductive, alluring, and stunning. Each of these perspectives help us understand what sexy is, but defining and knowing "sexy" often escapes one definitive concept. Why? Because each of us is unique and adopts a different vision and idea about sexiness.

Certainly, nuances exist, and what you find sexy naturally varies a bit from the next person. That's a good thing. Otherwise, we would all be seeking the same person while conforming to a norm. But at the same time, we can agree that specific features are appealing. For example, the cartoon character Jessica Rabbit is considered sexy for a reason…because she has many of the features we typically find sensually arousing. Shiny hair, a curvaceous figure, and long eyelashes are some of her most prominent attributes that we associate with being sexy. Not everyone, or even many, have this Sophía Vergara–like figure, however we all could benefit from optimizing our own unique features in a way that increases our confidence and external appeal.

When it comes to locking down what's sexy, the ultimate definition is certainly in the eye of the beholder. However, we know that certain features or traits consistently trigger positive emotions in us. For example, you might be attracted to a man who is more rugged in appearance while someone else finds a polished aristocrat more appealing. We also have individual preferences. But when comparing the two men, both could likely have the same square jawline, nice teeth, a muscular chest, beautiful wavy hair, and smooth, healthy skin. When it comes down to it…certain features are consistently sexy.

"People often say that 'beauty is in the eye of the beholder,' and I say that the most liberating thing about beauty is realizing that you are the beholder. This empowers us to find beauty in places where others have not dared to look, including inside ourselves." **Salma Hayek**[1]

Lucky for us, there is a wealth of information about human sexuality that we can call upon to assist in our understanding. Studies have shown that what we perceive as sexy is fairly consistent, and these findings have resulted in the advancement of specific fields of science. Hundreds of studies involving evolutionary psychology support the notion that many of the things we routinely find sexy relate to fertility and procreation. A small waist-to-hip ratio and larger breasts in women have been linked to sexual attractiveness and clearly support a fertility perspective. Men with a chiseled body and a strong jawline are presumed to have greater virility. And shiny hair, beautiful teeth, healthy skin, and a toned body are linked to youthfulness, which also implies enhanced fertility. Sexy features and beautiful features are often indistinguishable.

Behavioral psychology has found similar patterns when it comes to sexy. Flirtatiously playing with your hair draws attention to your face and highlights your more sensual attributes. A steady gaze with open eyes and long eyelashes creates a sense of trust and reliability, which supports a sexual relationship. Even color choices in clothing and lipstick have been linked to perceptions about sexual attractiveness or readiness by men who were studied gazing at their photos. This

---

1 The relentless conservative, "Something We Might Agree On: Beauty?" Huffington Post, 2011, retrieved from https://www.huffingtonpost.com/the-relentless-conservative/something-we-might-agree-_b_932870.html.

is how we harness subliminal messaging. Like our appearance, the way we behave also signals our level of health, fertility, virility, and youthfulness...and we will delve into what movements, actions, postures, etc. can be employed to send out a sexy vibe. Some are subtler than others; some may not feel like they fit you. We will discuss how to harness your best you by choosing which aspects feel right to you from the wealth of information in this book. Learning how to harness our movements and behaviors can bring out our inner sexy and call attention to our most attractive features.

You don't have to take science's word for it, though...look around. Why do you think many marketing ads depict young, vibrant men and women to promote their products? Have you noticed the increasing number of female sports reporters and weather casters who are quite aesthetically pleasing to the eye? It is no surprise that sex sells, but the key here is to see what sexy actually is. Women with narrow waists, relatively wider hips, youthful skin, and endearing eyes, and men with athletic physiques, broad shoulders, thick hair, and beautiful smiles are ubiquitously seen as sexy. From celebrities to supermodels to cartoons, pop culture repeatedly reinforces this simple message. We can spend time trying to resist the pressures placed by marketing or we can understand that the marketing responds to our evolutionary preferences. We as consumers decide which ads we respond to, and that is why we get more of those types of ads.

Throughout my career as a board-certified dermatologist specializing in cosmetic procedures, I have had the pleasure of helping a broad range of clients. As you can imagine, each of these individuals has had unique needs and perspectives, but over and over again, many of the views and opinions about what is sexy have remained consistent. Some of these people are icons of sexiness whom I have had the joy of becoming comfortable with and have seen in their casual, relaxed mode. These high-profile clients are sexy for a living and know how to go from ordinary chill to exceptional when they need to. I doubt these individuals have read studies on what is sexy, or taken behavioral science and marketing courses, but instinctively they have nailed down the sexy. And it turns out, the features they highlight when preparing for red carpet events are remarkably consistent with what the textbooks say. Putting together all that I have learned from studies, pop culture, and my personal experience, I will highlight which features are consistently appealing and how to best enhance them.

Would you like to be sexy? If you have picked up this book, you probably would. But then again, who wouldn't? This does not mean that we strive to be sexy all the time. While a few people seem to have mastered this achievement (Kim Kardashian comes to mind), we were not meant to exude sexiness twenty-four hours a day, seven days a week. That would be like eating chocolate at every meal. Though such a diet may sound good at first, the chocolate eventually loses some of its allure over time. Being sexy should therefore be considered a personal asset or a tool that you pick up and use when you need it.

Marilyn Monroe understood this concept all too well. Marilyn's friend Susan Strasberg recalls how Marilyn could walk through the streets of New York City being essentially unnoticed until she decided to shake things up. Marilyn would ask her friend, "Do you want to see me be her?" Within a few moments, Marilyn would make some inner adjustment, and suddenly crowds would then gather, recognizing the celebrity.[2] For Marilyn, sexy could be easily called upon whenever she deemed it appropriate, and likewise, she could put it away as well.

In the same way actresses repeatedly rehearse their lines and corporate executives study their markets, enhancing your abilities to be sexy allows you to be a bolder, more empowered person. As I have said, all of us are sexy because that is how we got here. It is a powerfully consistent trait in humans, because individuals who were not interested in sex would not have procreated. We are born with this power, and as we "grow up" as members of society, we learn to repress the sexy—to keep it on the back burner. We are squandering a good bit of personal power when we chronically do this and do not let our sexy, powerful side come out and play sometimes. For the vast majority of my clients, pursuits to be sexy are not driven by a need to fill an emotional void. Instead, they reflect specific efforts by people to improve themselves. Their underlying motivation to be sexy is simply self-improvement and self-empowerment.

In essence, sexy is both a state of mind and a state of being. It encompasses being beautiful both inside and out, and it allows the expression of one's self in an alluring way that attracts attention to our unique sensual features. What many fail to understand and *see* is that we are all sexy in our own way, and each of us has the power to unleash our sexiness whenever we choose to do so. A dedicated effort to take our beauty and confidence to the next level allows us

2 Susan Strasberg, *Marilyn and Me: Sisters, Rivals, Friends* (New York: Warner Books, 1992).

to truly realize our potential as an individual: "Beauty is being the best possible version of yourself on the inside and out."

Seven Days to Sexy is your seven-day, step-by-step plan that allows you to unleash your absolute sexiest self. By understanding what sexy is from scientific evidence as well as from your own personal experiences, you will acquire an in-depth knowledge about the specific goals you want to pursue. And by coupling this knowledge with proven real-world beauty tips and procedures, you will be able to realize these goals within a seven-day process while embarking on more long-term objectives in seven-week and seven-month plans as well. *Seven Days to Sexy* is your ultimate guide in taking your "sexy" to the next level.

And for those who have a bit more time to achieve sexiness, part two of this book includes plans for Seven Weeks to Sexy and Seven Months to Sexy.

Though the tips in this book can work for everyone, some may not be for you. However, through my experiences and interactions with hundreds of women, I have gained a wealth in pearls, tips, and tricks in the pursuit of sexiness and beauty. Indeed, the opportunity to listen to women's stories and perspectives has greatly enhanced my understanding of what features define being gorgeous and sexy, and how to achieve it. Between performing countless procedures and listening to my patients, I have learned many strategies that can help you attain your self-optimization goals in only a matter of days. Being sexy is something we all should enjoy from time to time, and having the real-world tools to achieve this is important when you are striving to be your very best. *Seven Days to Sexy* will provide you with these valuable and essential tools.

> *"Beauty is a kind of radiance. People who possess a true inner beauty, their eyes are a little brighter, their skin a little more dewy. They vibrate at a different frequency."*
> **Cameron Diaz**[3]

Seven Days to Sexy is essentially a beauty book. Beauty lies at the heart of sexy. When we feel beautiful, insecurities are lifted, and our ability to feel sexy grows significantly. When we perceive others as beautiful, sensual emotions may develop in the right contexts and circumstances. Therefore, this book is first and foremost a book that provides incredible beauty tips that enable you to become the sexiest person you can be. By recognizing the common beauty and behavioral features we associate with being sexy, we can define specific goals to work toward. And by revealing professional secrets used by supermodels and celebrities alike, you will be able to quickly attain these goals.

It's time to be empowered. It's time to be your absolute best. It's time to unleash your inner sexy.

---

3 Candice Graham, "How to feel beauty from within." *Healthscope Magazine*, n.d., retrieved from https://www.healthscopemag.com/health-scope/how-to-feel-beautiful-from-within/.

PART I

Understanding Sexy

We have all been there. Dressed to kill, fresh from the hairdresser, and excited about the evening ahead, your hips sway back and forth as you walk with a sense of unparalleled confidence. Men cannot help but turn their heads as you pass by, with many keeping their gaze well after you have walked past. Every encounter you have seems to go extremely well. Lobby doormen rush to open the door for you. Store attendants bend over backward to ensure your every whim is met. Even your barista flirtatiously smiles as he gives you your grande latte. These are moments to be relished, without a doubt.

In those moments, we project an aura of sexiness that gets everyone's attention. Whether we consciously intend to do so at the time might be hard to say, but all the same, those around us have no problem knowing it. By all accounts, we are being sexy. But we must ask... what is it that is creating such a sensual glow? Is it our appearance? Is it the way we move? Is it something intangible that is difficult to define? In a word...yes. Having an alluring appeal involves all these things, which makes trying to pin it down somewhat challenging. But simply because the definition of sexy is a bit evasive doesn't mean it can't be demystified.

"To me, 'sexy' is a kind of beauty, a kind of self-expression, one that is to be celebrated." **Emily Ratajkowski**[4]

Over the course of time, many have tried to figure out exactly what determines beauty and attractiveness. Some have identified certain looks and appearances that are commonly associated with sexiness. Others have looked at specific behaviors that tend to evoke enchanted gazes. And some have sought to examine the state of mind associated with a sensual demeanor. All these pursuits have provided us with some remarkable insights into sexiness, and appreciating these insights can certainly help us be our sexiest self. Understanding these ideas can also help us turn our sexy "on" whenever we so desire.

While we could provide a brief, concrete definition of sexiness, such an approach fails to give justice to all the features associated with being irresistibly attractive. This would be like trying to explain your love life in a single phrase without going into all the delicious complexities. How unsatisfying that would be! We would want to hear all the juicy details. Similarly, we have to look from different perspectives to understand exactly what makes us desirable. Sexy isn't simply a look, a walk, or an attitude...it is all of these plus much more. If we want to unleash our sensual side, we need to take a much deeper look into everything that it involves.

We will thus examine in this section several features that create that aura of sexiness we individually desire to portray. Whether it's

4 *Huh Magazine*, "Emily Ratajkowski Writes About Her Childhood and What It Means to Be Sexy," n.d., retrieved from http://www.huhmagazine.co.uk/11226/emily-ratajkowski-writes-about-her-childhood-and-what-it-means-to-be-sexy.

our appearance, our behavior, or our frame of mind, each offers opportunities to show our sexiest selves. In fact, each of these three influences the others. Frame of mind affects behavior and appearances, and conversely appearances and behavior can lead to a certain frame of mind, and so on. I have witnessed these complex relationships firsthand through hundreds of clients regardless whether they were supermodels or CEOs. Science supports this point of view as well. Dozens of research studies highlight how many of the features associated with attractiveness are consistent across cultures and are linked to our evolutionary history as human beings. So, let's examine these features from a deeper perspective...not only will it be more fun, but it will also give us a much better definition of what sexy is.

Chapter 1

Looking Sexy

"I'm a bad good girl. Every girl likes feeling hot and sexy and beautiful—and likes hearing it." **Hayden Panettiere**[5]

When someone mentions the word "sexy," what comes to mind? Perhaps you envision a certain celebrity or supermodel. Maybe your last passionate encounter pops into your head. If you're like most people, you probably recall specific features that person had...their hair, their eyes, their physique. In short, you likely visualized how beautiful and appealing they were. And why wouldn't you? After all, what we see is rich with information. A picture paints a thousand words if not a million, so it makes perfect sense that our first thoughts about sexiness invite specific images of people we find incredibly sensual and attractive.

What about those moments when you personally felt irresistible? You likely recall the look of another's passionate desire (saucer-like eyes and slack jaw) that you evoked as he hoped to devour you. In that moment, you enjoyed a confident feeling of sexual power that came from your ability to elicit this reaction. How you looked, felt,

5 *Cosmopolitan Magazine*, "The hot things celebs tell Cosmo," 2011, retrieved from https://www.cosmopolitan.com/entertainment/celebs/news/g1326/sexy-quotes-from-cosmo-cover-girls/.

and acted is what it took to drive him crazy and fill him with an insatiable attraction to you — not to mention that *je ne sais quoi*. Men, in particular, are aroused by what they see, and we often feel our sexiest when we recognize the allure we provoke.

Let's break down this visual a bit further, shall we? Certainly, someone's entire persona as well as their image can portray sexiness, but at the same time, this image is composed of many individual parts. Hair color, hair length, and even hairstyles can affect whether we perceive someone as desirable or not. A dashing smile and beautifully smooth skin can similarly make an impression. Eye color and eyelashes are known to be a focus of sensual attraction. And everyone knows a shapely figure can cause heads to turn up and down the block. Similar to that Fendi handbag created with every exquisite detail considered, what you perceive as visually enticing is a constellation of many wonderful parts.

This gives us our first clue about how to unleash our sexy. In order to become our most attractive and desirable self, the goal is to create our own personal masterpiece. But in doing so, we will need to focus on different parts of our palette. In pursuing the artistry of sexy, we will be using mixed media involving our hair, our eyes, our smile, and much more. Of course, your masterpiece will be unique and different from anyone else's. But at the same time, you can learn specific techniques to help you along your way. Some colors might be better choices than others, and some shapes and styles might be more provocative on you. This is where both science and my own professional insights can help.

Starting at the Top – Sexy Hair

When it comes to being our most desirable, hair certainly matters. Men and women alike spend a great deal of time making sure their hair is properly groomed, colored, and maintained so they can present themselves in the most desirable way. This trend starts early in our lives, as we are all familiar with the many hours we spent as teens in front of a mirror making sure our hair was exactly the way we wanted it. We even have an easy way to let others know about our frustrations when our hair won't cooperate. "Sorry I was late…I am having a bad hair day."

So, it's a given that we all appreciate how our hair can play a role in how we feel and how others perceive us. Therefore, what type of hair do you think men prefer? Judging by television and Internet ads, you would likely guess that women with long, wavy, blonde hair have a stronghold on the market. To some extent, this may be true. Hair should be shiny, healthy, and flowing, not motionless or sprayed into place. Silky, smooth hair is always in. Frizzy, dry hair is always out. But having attractive hair goes beyond these simple assessments. In order to appreciate what it is that makes someone perceive your hair as irresistible, we need to dig a little deeper.

Let's first start with hair color. Is it true that blonde hair tends to be more attractive to most men? Interestingly, the answer is yes… sometimes. In a research study that involved over 650 European men, each were shown various photograph sets of women with either red, blonde, or brown hair. When the researchers tallied the results, they found that most men found the women with blonde hair to be more attractive than those with either red or brown hair.[6] So, there you have it…blondes are sexier.

Hold on…not so fast! As mentioned, the study was conducted in Europe where most men typically have darker hair and skin tones. One of the explanations why these men preferred blondes relates to a (subconscious) human attraction to others who are inherently different. Why would this be? Because diversity is important when it comes to the health of our families and our species. From an evolutionary point of view, having children with someone genetically different from us helps avoid many unfortunate illnesses and diseases. We certainly don't go out and say, "Wow! His DNA profile seems really different from mine. What a turn-on!" But at the same time, we are subconsciously attracted to these features.

As it turns out, hair color itself is less important when compared to other features involving your hair. While different shades of natural hair colors affect our appeal, men typically are not attracted to unusual colors like pink or blue. When we think of sensual hairstyles, we tend to think about people who have shiny, flowing hair. How many boys (and men!) in the late 1970s didn't have a poster or photograph of Farrah Fawcett in that red bikini? We will come back to that red bikini, her dazzling smile, and her shapely physique in a bit when we discuss the specific effects our shape, facial expressions, and clothing have on sex appeal. But for now, you can appreciate that her feathered

---

6 Zinnia J. Janif, Robert C. Brooks, and Barnaby J. Dixson, "Are preferences for women's hair color frequency-dependent?" *Adaptive Human Behavior and Physiology* 1, no. 1 (2015): 54–71.

blonde hair with bouncy curls took center stage. For that matter, what woman didn't want to imitate her iconic hairstyle? At that time, and for decades to follow, Farrah's hair was synonymous with sexy.

> "*God gave women intuition and femininity. Used properly, the combination easily jumbles the brain of any man I've ever met.*" **Farrah Fawcett**[7]

Though Farrah may not be the sex symbol most men think of today, other equally beautiful women have taken her place. The Kardashians have certainly played this role for many, and their long, dark shiny hair is synonymous with sensual desire. Likewise, past icons like Raquel Welch or Elizabeth Taylor had similarly alluring hair but with a completely different style. While science has not studied hair length and sexual appeal to a great extent, longer, flowing hair on a woman has been associated with higher attractiveness ratings among men in some studies.[8] Throughout time, this hairstyle has most consistently been linked to male preference.

So, what was it that made Farrah's hair (and these other sexual icons) so irresistibly attractive? If you look at various studies, researchers suggest that it all has to do with two key things...health and youth. Suppose you're a caveman back in the Stone Age. You may have been attracted to women of varying ages, but you were most likely to successfully carry on your family lineage when selecting healthier,

---

7 Norman M. Brown and Ellen S. Amatea, *Love and intimate relationships: Journeys of the heart* (New York: Routledge, 2013).

8 Jodi Manning, "The sociology of hair: Hair symbolism among college students," *Social Sciences Journal* 10, no. 1 (2010): 11.

more fertile women. As a result, a preference for features that were connected to wellness developed over time. In the same way genetic diversity can help increase the chances of having healthy children, so can a mother who is in good health.

As it turns out, hair can say a lot about one's level of health. What we eat affects the caliber and appearance of our hair. After all, we are what we eat! For example, a high-protein diet provides amino acids and other nutrients that keep the keratin in our hair strong. The same is true of vitamins and other micronutrients. Conversely, illnesses adversely affect how our hair looks. Vitamin deficiencies and hormonal disorders such as thyroid disease can result in brittle, thin, stringy hair. Thus, hair that is long, shiny, thick, and flowing epitomizes what is normally defined as a healthy glow. And that is sexy!

The link between our hair's appearance and overall health is also linked to a youthful hormonal profile. A woman's fertility is noted to peak between her early twenties through her midthirties.[9] During this time, our hair is at its best. As we grow older, our hair naturally becomes thinner, more brittle, and coarser, replacing the more robust, shiny hair we likely had in our youth. In general, higher estrogen levels provide for faster-growing, shiny hair. From our caveman's point of view, a woman with long, thick, flowing hair is more likely to be in her most reproductive years. It only seems logical that this would be an attractive (and sexually desirable) feature. It certainly

---

9 Jan Antfolk, Benny Salo, Katarina Alanko, Emilia Bergen, Jukka Corander, N. Kenneth Sandnabba, and Pekka Santtila, "Women's and men's sexual preferences and activities with respect to the partner's age: evidence for female choice," Evolution and Human Behavior 36, no. 1 (2015): 73–79.

makes more sense than needing his mate to have long hair so he could drag her around!

In theory, the link between sexiness and healthy and youthful hair seems intuitive, and science supports this association. In one study involving ninety men, researchers observed how likely men were to help a woman who had accidentally dropped a glove on the ground. The same woman performed all three phases of the experiment, but in each phase, she wore a different hairstyle. In one phase, she had a ponytail; in another, a hair bun; and in the third, her hair fell naturally below her shoulders. Interestingly enough, men were significantly more likely to come to her aid when her hairstyle was more natural (and youthful).[10]

When it comes to looking attractive, hair matters. This is not to say that you may not have incredible sex appeal with shorter hairstyles or with an array of hair colors. The key, however, is maintaining a healthy and youthful look regardless of the style or color you choose. You can achieve this goal in a number of ways with some effort on your part. There are both short-term and long-term solutions for achieving full glossy locks. Taking advantage of the beauty tips regarding your hair in the *Seven Days to Sexy* plan can greatly help you project your sexiest self.

Facing the Facts – Eyes, Eyebrows, and Lips

It's no secret that our initial attraction to another person begins with our facial appearance. We are told to put our best face forward...and when

10 Nicolas Guéguen, "Women's hairstyle and men's behavior: A field experiment," *Scandinavian Journal of Psychology* 56, no. 6 (2015): 637–640.

it comes to being sexy, this is good advice. Why? Because we ascertain a great deal of information about someone simply from their facial features. You may realize you're quite attracted to another person's eye color and smile, but you may be less aware of your subconscious perceptions about that person's facial symmetry, contrasts, and other less obvious features. All these facial characteristics are important when it comes to physical (and often emotional) attraction.

Let's consider facial symmetry to start. Believe it or not, the degree of symmetry we perceive in another's face tells us a lot about that person. Did you ever wonder why you intuitively spend so much time making sure your eyebrows are even and of the same shape? Or why evenly applied makeup or eye shadow matters so much? The answer is symmetry. Symmetry is a subconscious cue that we are healthy and well.[11] As human beings, we immediate make snap judgements about such things during those first few seconds we encounter another person. Symmetry equals health; health equals good reproductive potential; fertility equals sexual desire…in short, symmetry affects our perception of what (and who) is most desirable.

Of course, facial symmetry is only one piece of the puzzle. What does science say about our eyes when it comes to attractiveness and sensual desire? The eyes are a bit more complex, and perhaps they should be since they are the "windows to our soul." Surveys have indicated that most men look at a woman's eyes first when sizing up their level of attraction. The more open the eyes are, the more

---

11 Ian D. Stephen and K. W. Tan, "Healthy body, healthy face? Evolutionary approaches to attractiveness perception," In *Culture and cognition: A collection of critical essays*, Peter Lang International Publishers, 2015.

dilated the pupil, and the steadier the gaze, the more likely men are to find the woman sensually appealing. In contrast, narrower eyes with small pupils and an erratic gaze have the opposite effect. Thus, the shape and "look" of our eyes can make a significant difference in our aura of sexiness.

Why might this be true? For one, open eyes and a steady gaze imply interest as well as trustworthiness. Think about it...the best villains in films and cartoons alike often have small, beady eyes with a shifty gaze. It is very difficult to trust someone like that. Because we often have only a few seconds to make a quick assessment of others, we look to their eyes to get some idea if they can be trusted. While being sexy implies passion, desire, and seduction, it also requires a significant level of trust. We naturally tend to lose interest in someone if we become skeptical about their intentions.

Trustworthiness is not the only thing that makes widely opened eyes appealing. Eyes that appear more open, including those with more dilated pupils, tend to project an image of youthfulness as well as sexual interest. Centuries ago, women used belladonna opioids to dilate their pupils in order to appear more attractive. Likewise, in the course of sexual pleasure, the hormone oxytocin is released, which causes the pupils to dilate and a person to feel greater emotional sensitivity.[12] In essence, wide eyes are subconscious cues of receptiveness and desire. The more pronounced our eyes appear, the more attractive we become.

---

12 Siri Leknes, Johan Wessberg, Dan-Mikael Ellingsen, Olga Chelnokova, Håkan Olausson, and Bruno Laeng, "Oxytocin enhances pupil dilation and sensitivity to 'hidden'emotional expressions," *Social Cognitive and Affective Neuroscience* 8, no. 7 (2012): 741–749.

Think about that adorable puppy you saw a few weeks ago. Besides having a smooth, velvety coat of fur, it also had endearing eyes that melted you the moment you saw them. While our eyes reach their adult size rather quickly, the rest of our facial features and head in general continue to grow well into our twenties. Likewise, aging tends to cause the soft tissues behind and around the eye to shrink, resulting in an appearance of smaller eyes. Thus, when the eye-to-face ratio is higher, we instinctively associate this appearance with youthfulness. Here again, from an evolutionary perspective, this youthful appearance suggests greater reproductive potential, and we naturally find this more desirable and appealing as a result.

Along with youthfulness comes healthiness, and healthy-appearing eyes are important. Have you ever come across someone with bloodshot eyes? How about someone whose eyes are jaundiced or yellowish in color? We naturally associate such eyes with poor health, and as a result, we tend to view them as less than attractive. In contrast, we associate clear, white eyes with health and alertness. Paying attention to how your eyes look reflects an important part of enhancing your beauty. Making sure you get adequate sleep, and carrying around some Visine when this isn't possible, might be a good strategy.

While we may all want to have doe eyes like Penelope Cruz, Audrey Hepburn, and Mila Kunis, not all of us are so endowed. But that doesn't mean we can't enhance our own eyes with an incredibly sexy look. One of the ways we accomplish this is by bringing attention to our eyes by contrasting them with other parts of our face. Dark or colorful contrasts in our facial features around the eyes naturally serve to augment the appearance of our eyes themselves. Long, thick eyelashes...dark, perfectly arched eyebrows...artfully applied eyeliner and shadow. Cleopatra knew this all too well. All of these serve to draw attention to one of your most alluring attributes...your eyes.

Even high-arched cheekbones, or the appearance of such, help make your eyes more pronounced and attractive. At the same time, these facial features also provide clues about youthfulness. As we age, the bone volumes of our cheekbones as well as the bones around our teeth and gums become smaller in size. Similarly, muscles used for chewing and expression become smaller as well. The overall effect is to take away from the smooth, curvaceous and symmetric appearance of a woman's youthful face while making the eyes less pronounced. Combine this with subtle wrinkles around the eyes and mouth, and the appearance of youthfulness gradually fades. However, minimizing these subtle features offers wonderful opportunities to enhance our beauty and attractiveness with relatively little effort.

While our eyes play a role in communicating trust, interest, and youthfulness, eyebrows also have more than one role in enhancing our sexiness and beauty. As noted, eyebrows provide a sense of facial symmetry, which implies good health and well-being. Likewise, eyebrows can be used to help highlight our eyes through proper contrast. But our eyebrows also convey information about health. Aging and hormone changes cause brow hairs to become lighter and thinner, whereas youthful brows are thick and dark. Eyebrows above the upper bony ridge of the eye imply youthfulness and reproductive potential. And once again, what is perceived as attractive and beautiful correlates with the more youthful look.

Later in this book, we will discuss a number of effective procedures, products, and techniques for enhancing the beauty of your eyebrows. We will also provide important do's and don'ts regarding the eyebrows. Likewise, we will cover techniques to promote a healthier (and more attractive) appearance of your eyes by enhancing their whiteness and clarity. In both cases, these approaches seek to augment a healthy and youthful appearance, and in the process, help create a more desirable and appealing look. You might not have instinctively associated health and youth with sexy, but these themes are in fact related to our overall appearance.

As you can see, our faces provide a wealth of information and cues about health, wellness, and youthfulness. Each of these is associated with increased fertility, and simply from an evolutionary perspective, you can appreciate why these features have been attractive and desirable since the beginning of time. But these sexy cues are not the only ones associated with a woman's reproductive capacity. Some facial features are more directly linked to telltale signs of sexuality.

> *"Beauty, to me, is about being comfortable in your own skin. That, or a kick-ass red lipstick."* **Gwyneth Paltrow**[13]

What is it about plump, tantalizing lips that attracts a man? From a sexy point of view, certainly lips can be alluring while inviting a

---

13 Bellable, "Gwyneth Paltrow: Beauty to me, is about being comfortable in your own skin, That… or a kick-ass red lipstick," 2017, retrieved from https://bellable.com/extra/gwyneth-paltrow-beauty-comfortable-skin-kick-ass-red-lipstick/.

passionate kiss. From a psychological perspective, Freud might suggest this has to do with an oral fixation left over from childhood, while others have suggested enhanced redness might occur in the lips and cheeks during ovulation.[14] But from an evolutionary standpoint, full, juicy, sensual lips are linked to higher levels of estrogen. You got it… luscious lips are synonymous with fertility.

At first, you might think this is just some recent trend that began in the States a few decades back. But did you know, lip enlargement rituals date back centuries in various parts of the world?[15] Ancient cultures in Egypt, Africa, and the Amazon all performed cultural ceremonies involving enhancement of the lips.[16] While we have become more adept at enhancing this erogenous part of our faces, lips have always been associated with sensual desire. From lip liner to lip gloss, and from lipstick to lip enhancers, the pursuit of full, moist, sensual lips continues as we desire to be as sexy as possible.

The appearance of our facial features can make a tremendous impact on how we are perceived. What is interesting is that much of our assessment lies beneath our conscious mind. We subconsciously detect subtle cues that suggest health, wellness, youthfulness, and fertility, and from these, we make judgments about what is sexy and what is not. While many parts of the body showcase sexiness and beauty, the face is unique in that it offers a quick chance to assess our

---

14 Andrew J. Elliot and Adam D. Pazda, "Dressed for sex: Red as a female sexual signal in humans," *PLoS One* 7, 4 (2012): e34607.
15 Desmond Morris, *The naked woman: A study of the female body* (New York: Macmillan, 2007).
16 Victoria Pitts-Taylor, ed., *Cultural Encyclopedia of the Body [2 volumes]*, ABC-CLIO, 2008.

level of attraction to someone else. Why wouldn't we want to make the most of this opportunity?

The Devil's in the Details—Sexy Skin and Nails

As you know all too well, physical attraction does not stop at the neck. While that first sensual impression often starts when our eyes meet another's, these initial opportunities offer invitations to take a little longer gaze and check out "the whole package" (so to speak). The appearance of our skin says a lot about us in this regard. Understandably, we spend a great deal of time taking proper care of our skin so we can have that healthy, youthful glow. In fact, the skin care market alone exceeds $127 billion. If you didn't think of skin as sexy before, you should definitely reconsider your position.

What makes skin sexy? Despite concerns about the risks of skin cancer associated with sun exposure, having a healthy tan remains an attractive feature. Surveys have shown that both men and women prefer a tanned look, both for themselves and for others. Why for themselves? Because they consider a healthy tan to make them sexier in their appearance…and they are right (according to the survey).[17] However, a tan glow has its downside. Sun exposure causes many skin problems (including skin cancer) and damages skin, undermining our efforts in pursuing beautiful skin. For example, too much sun leads to a leathery texture in addition to premature wrinkling and other blemishes. Likewise, aging "brown" spots begin to occur with sun

17 Marita Broadstock, Ron Borland, and Robyn Gason, "Effects of suntan on judgements of healthiness and attractiveness by adolescents," *Journal of Applied Social Psychology* 22, no. 2 (1992): 157–172.

tanning, as does an increase in freckles. While worshiping the sun can provide you with the tan you seek, you are likely stealing from your future to pay for the present.

Why are we so enamored with a good tan? What is it about a bronzed glow that arouses our senses? Some suggest a good tan is perceived as being healthy. Pale skin is linked to certain conditions like poor nutrition and low blood counts. Likewise, pale skin suggests a vulnerability to sun exposure, since fair-skinned individuals have higher rates of skin cancer. And the pigment in the skin (made of substances like melanin and carotenoids) have been shown to help protect us from disease.[18] By boosting our immune system and by helping protect us from the sun's rays, these pigments inherently imply better health...and healthy is sexy.

On the other hand, we should consider the strong influence of trends. Tanned skin was not always found to be the most attractive. During Victorian times and other eras, pale skin was more appealing. Pallor was associated with better health and well-being since only the working class was exposed to long periods of sunlight. In addition to powdering their faces, some women even took arsenic to achieve a paler skin appearance.

With the Farrah Fawcett era came the dawn of the tan beauty trend. Suntans became associated with greater time for pleasure and leisure, which in turn signaled greater wealth and security. Unfortunately, the damage from this trend is what I clean up every day in the form of

---

18 I. D. Stephen, V. Coetzee, & D. I. Perrett, D. I., "Carotenoid and melanin pigment coloration affect perceived human health," *Evolution and Human Behavior* 32, no. 3 (2011), 216–227.

skin cancer excisions and laser treatments. Despite better alternatives such as self-tanning lotions and procedures, excessive sun exposure still occurs quite often. However, it seems the pendulum has swung the other way, and we are now somewhere in the middle. People now tend to understand the dangers of sun exposure, so they practice moderation and sunscreen use.

Of course, the color of our skin tone is not the only factor when it comes to an attractive appearance. Someone may have a wonderfully tanned look, but dry skin, uneven color, and subtle wrinkles undermine the overall impression. Skin should look well-hydrated and natural, in addition to having a healthy glow. Why? Because we associate smooth, radiant skin with youthfulness as well as health, and these again play a role in defining beauty and sexiness. Smooth, clear skin is what we typically find most appealing. Skin that is free of pimples and pustules...skin that is soft and wrinkle free...these define beauty.

You might wonder if some skin conditions might be associated to a greater extent with youth. Specifically, acne is often associated with teens, and based on our youthfulness hypothesis, these individuals might be found to be more attractive. As it turns out, this is not the case. In studies surveying men and women, the participants did estimate the age of individuals with acne as being younger than images of those without acne. However, when it came to attractiveness, the opposite was true.[19] Those with clearer skin came out ahead. In essence, healthy-appearing skin wins out over youthful skin when push comes to shove.

---

19 Richard M. Timms, "Moderate acne as a potential barrier to social relationships: Myth or reality?" *Psychology, Health & Medicine* 18, no. 3 (2013): 310–320.

Given these insights about what makes skin beautiful and desirable, think about some of the fantasy films of late. Zoe Saldana played the sexy, exotic love interest in both *Guardians of the Galaxy* films and in *Avatar.* In one, her skin was colored a less-than-appealing shade of green, and in the other, a vibrant yet anemic color of blue. Neither of these colors would typically be considered sexy, but somehow, Saldana pulled it off. How? Because she has great skin. Her smooth, well-hydrated, healthy-appearing skin offered a more sensual impression of attractiveness that outweighed any negative effects the unusual skin color might have had.

Certainly, the skin of our face can make a powerful impression, but at the same time, our hands also can be influential in this regard. I have heard on more than one occasion that the best way to tell a person's actual age is to look at their hands. Why? Because often our hands reveal skin that is more weathered and wrinkled as we age. And dry skin, abrasions, and even rashes on our hands can offer insights about our health and hygiene. Here again, beauty is associated with smooth skin free of any blemishes or evidences of aging. And like the rest of our skin, our hands deserve attention in this regard if we want to be our most desirable.

If we want to look appealing, we need to take good care of our skin. The appearance of our skin provides some insights into our youthfulness and health, and this can either enhance or detract from the sexy look we are trying to achieve. Similarly, the appearance of our nails offers the same opportunities. As an extension of our skin, our nails also reflect our overall level of health while giving us an opportunity to shine. You might be amazed at the impact your fingernails and toenails have in creating your sexy persona.

What comes to mind when you think of sexy nails? Long, colorful nails perfectly manicured (or pedicured)? This would be consistent with what most people see as sexy. But what some women fail to realize is that this look has less to do with running your nails across his skin or through his hair and more to do with how healthy your nails appear. Did you know your nails are a good indication of good or bad health? Nail infections are not uncommon, and these can cause nail discoloration, irregularities in shape, or more brittle nails. Poor nutrition can also result in telltale signs in your nails. A lack of iron, calcium, and zinc can result in more brittle nails or pale discolorations. And poor circulation can also affect nail appearance and health.

The shape of your nails is also important. Despite what some Hollywood images portray at times, most men think the sexiest nails are those that are moderate in length, nicely curved, and smooth in appearance. Excessively long, pointed, exotic nails might trigger thoughts of an extremely passionate encounter, but men don't necessarily see this as being the most attractive over time.[20] Why might this be? Because the moderate shape is more natural and provides a more consistent image of good health.

Therefore, the overall color, shape, and symmetry of your fingernails and toenails can say a lot about your level of wellness. This helps explain why meticulously cared-for natural colored nails can portray

---

20 *Cosmopolitan*, "Three nail trends men love," 2010, retrieved from http://www.cosmopolitan.com/style-beauty/beauty/how-to/a8737/nail-trends-men-love/.

sexiness. By highlighting these same features in shape and beauty that are intuitively associated with good health, your nails naturally project an attractive appearance to others. Certainly, beauty is more than skin deep, but when making that first sexy impression, paying attention to your skin and nails is important.

The Timeless Hourglass—The Perpetual Sexy Shape

If we think about a shapely physique, a sexy look likely reflects our impression of what we see most commonly in society around us. Who do you envision when you think about a perfectly sexy body? Do you think about Sofia Vergara or Beyoncé? Do their hourglass figures symbolize the sexy shape men desire? Certainly, the way our bodies look (or the shape they have) is not the only factor when it comes to being sexy, but paying attention to our physique is important nonetheless. Throughout the course of time, the hourglass figure has consistently depicted what most men find attractive...and for good reason.

There is more than one way to characterize the hourglass figure. In decades past, the ideal female shape was described based on classic chest, waist, and hip measurements...the classic 36–24–36–inch dimensions have been immortalized in some of pop culture's history (the song "Brick House" comes to mind). Other depictions of the perfect hourglass figure have invaded other genres like cartoons, anime, and video games. Jessica Rabbit is well known by most, and for the gamers out there, *Lara Croft: Tomb Raider* epitomizes the stereotypical sexy build. Despite the exaggerated features in these portrayals, the perpetual image is pervasive everywhere we look when it comes to the sexy shape.

Even scientists have gotten involved in defining the exact shape of the most attractive female figure. But as you might guess, their approach is a bit more formal. Instead of citing specific circumferences or drawing caricatures, they have used a calculation known as the waist-to-hip ratio, or WTH ratio for short. Interestingly, many studies have been conducted looking at this ratio and its association with attractiveness. Regardless of the culture, most societies studied have shown incredible consistency when it comes to waist size versus hip size. In fact, some have found that the ideal WTH ratio is about 0.7.[21] In other words, men found women the most attractive and sexy when their waists were about 70 percent the size of their hips.

What is it about these unique measurements of our waist and hips that make us look so sexy? As you might have guessed by now, an ideal WTH ratio also says a great deal about health and reproductive potential. For example, a higher WTH ratio is associated with several poor health conditions. Naturally, obesity affects this ratio, but likewise, conditions like diabetes, heart disease, high blood pressure, and even cancer are more common among women who have higher waist to hip size. At the same time, female hormones like estrogen, which correlates with greater reproductive potential, result in lower WTH ratios. And youthfulness similarly has lower WTH ratios on average. You might have suspected the hourglass figure was constructed from

21 Charlene Moser, "Waist-to-Hip Ratio in Women and its Effect on Visual Processing and Attractiveness Ratings. A Behavioral and Electroencephalography Study," PhD diss., University of Geneva, 2015.

social trends alone, but in fact, this universal sexy shape is much more engrained on the male psyche from an evolutionary point of view.

Interestingly, the size of a woman's waist is the key determining factor when it comes to perceived beauty and attractiveness. In a sizable study, university students were asked to judge levels of attractiveness of three samples of women who had different waist and hip sizes. The three samples included college women, Playboy Playmates, and female cartoon characters. The researchers concluded that a smaller waist was what correlated the best with perceived attractiveness, while hip size did not.[22] Since hips can be more challenging to change, this research highlights how we can augment our physiques to be more appealing.

So, from a sexiness perspective, a smaller waist and proportionately larger hips are considered the most desirable. But what about breast size? Looking at pop culture, social trends have varied over the recent past. Breast augmentation is still popular, but at the same time, breast size reduction is similarly preferred by some women. Based on what we have learned about other aspects of beauty and sexiness, we would expect that breasts portray youthfulness, health, and fertility. Therefore, men should tend to perceive larger breasts as sexier. If we examine the specifics, this conjecture is fairly true.

Larger breast size is typically associated with higher estrogen levels, and thus, a link between breast size and higher levels of fertility makes sense. However, surveys of men from a variety of cultures tend to prefer medium-sized breasts more often than larger ones,

22 William D. Lassek and Steven JC Gaulin, "What makes Jessica Rabbit sexy? Contrasting roles of waist and hip size," *Evolutionary Psychology* 14, no. 2 (2016): 1474704916643459.

and all men preferred firmer breasts.[23] In considering these findings, something should be said about a natural look. While larger breasts are associated with enhanced reproductive capabilities, this likely only applies to a degree. Once proportions are overly exaggerated, a sense of unnaturalness may undermine the sexy look we are trying to achieve. They key is to pursue a figure that highlights breast firmness while maintaining an hourglass figure proportionate to your overall body size and shape.

When considering a sexy shape, evidence supports the hourglass figure as the most desirable. This does not necessarily mean your chest, waist, and hips need to be specific dimensions, and it does not mean your other features are less important. This evidence is simply provided so that you can make a more informed choice when it comes to your appearance. This might affect the clothes you wear, the activities in which you participate, or many other decisions. Certainly, one does not have to have an hourglass figure to be irresistibly attractive. It is simply one of many features that culminate in an aura of sexiness that you may or may not consider when it comes to your own personal preferences.

As the saying goes, you only get one shot at making a first impression. When it comes to sexy, this is certainly true. Our mental filters have been trained over many centuries to quickly assess and recognize specific looks that are instinctively appealing. And we've been doing our own research and discovering what works, but hopefully this

23 Jan Havlíček, Vít Třebický, Jaroslava Varella Valentova, Karel Kleisner, Robert Mbe Akoko, Jitka Fialová, Rosina Jash et al., "Men's preferences for women's breast size and shape in four cultures," *Evolution and Human Behavior* 38, no. 2 (2017): 217–226.

chapter has given a bit of insight as to why certain things do and can help you add to your arsenal of ideas. The good news is that we can easily embrace a sexy look simply by understanding the key features that are considered the most attractive and desirable. Better yet, you can achieve these qualities in a short amount of time. The seven-day plan will set you on your way to optimizing your appearance and unleashing your sexiest self.

Chapter 2
Sexy Moves

"What makes someone really sexy—and you can feel it when they talk to you or even just when they walk into a room—is the sense that they know they have something to contribute. They might be funny, smart, or really kind, but they know it, and when someone has that strong sense of self-worth, it's really sexy." **Eva Mendes**[24]

Do you remember the last time you were passionately attracted to someone but couldn't put your finger on why? He may have been a complete stranger, and his appearance may have not been mesmerizing in any specific way. Regardless, you found your desire for him almost irresistible. Was it the way he glanced in your direction? Perhaps it was a smile, the way he laughed, or the way he carried himself when he moved across the room. Something about him seemed purposeful, or intense, or perhaps simply poised. His movements gave suggestions about his confidence and abilities. The bottom line was that you found him incredibly sexy, and you wanted to get to know him better. The

24 *Shape Magazine*, "What makes celebs feel sexy," n.d., retrieved from https://www.shape.com/celebrities/celebrity-photos/what-makes-celebs-feel-sexy.

exact reasons you found him so attractive were probably not at the forefront of your mind at the time.

Looking beautiful is certainly important when you want to be your sexiest, but at the same time, the way you move can have powerful effects on others' level of attraction to you. Your appearance conveys a great deal of information about you—your youthfulness, your health, your personality, your energy, and much more. But similarly, your behavior communicates additional insights about these same features. When you act and move in a manner that is perceived as attractive (whether you do this on purpose or not), you enhance your sexual appeal. So, it makes perfect sense for you to better appreciate these subtleties in behavior that can be used to your advantage.

Unlike verbal communications, nonverbal cues can highlight a variety of personal attributes that others find attractive (or unattractive). The way you gaze or glance at others, the way you touch or gesture, the way you walk, and the body posture you choose are all rich in information. In fact, the amount of information you communicate through these nonverbal behaviors often far exceeds what you say or how you look. When you decide to "turn your sexy on," adopting some of these behaviors comes quite naturally and is intuitive. But you can also learn to invoke specific behaviors when you choose to to intentionally be even more attractive. How great is that?

In this chapter, we will explore those behaviors that have been shown to be most appealing. From eye contact and batting your eyes to a variety of flirtatious mannerisms, you will gain a much better understanding about how you can not only *look* beautiful but also *act* attractive. Sensual beauty is not limited to appearance alone but instead is a package deal. How you act provides powerful signals about confidence, interests, and your desirability. Though many perceive beauty as being only skin deep, nothing could be further from the truth. How you behave allows you to effectively express your beauty as well.

The Eyes Have It!

As quoted by Audrey Hepburn, "The beauty of a woman must be seen from in her eyes, because that is the doorway to her heart, the place where love resides."[25] Much can be said about the allure of beautiful eyes from the perspective of how they look. But when it comes to being attractive, how your eyes look is only a piece of the puzzle. In fact, the way we gaze and look at others is second only to our smile when it comes to provocative behaviors that enhance our attractiveness.[26] You can appreciate why this might be something you would want to know more about.

We have all seen two lovers immersed in each other's gaze, extending a long, persistent stare into one another's eyes. But for most other encounters, such a long-lasting look would likely be quite uncomfortable (if not downright creepy). We can distinguish eye contact into two specific areas...the glance and the gaze. While the quick glance can

---

25 N.a., "Audrey Hepburn quotes," Goodreads.com, 2017, retrieved from https://www.goodreads.com quotes/652699-the-beauty-of-a-woman-must-be-seen-from-in.
26 Caroline de Deus Tupinambá Rodrigues, Romeu Magnani, Maria Salete Candido Machado, and Osmir Batista Oliveira Jr., "The perception of smile attractiveness: variations from esthetic norms, photographic framing and order of presentation," *The Angle Orthodontist* 79, no. 4 (2009): 634–639.

be easy to recognize as a flirtatious behavior, knowing how to use the gaze in the most appealing way may be less intuitive. The casual peek across the room can provoke immediate interest, but the preferred duration and extent of eye contact in a conversation with someone can be more difficult to predict. Fortunately, we have science to help us out in these areas.

When it comes to direct eye contact with another person, the spectrum of a prolonged gaze can extend from one that signals interest and confidence to one that is more dominating and intimidating. Naturally, when we want to be our sexiest and most appealing, the latter is not the look we are going for. So, how long should we direct our gaze into another's eyes? According to some studies, most people make direct eye contact between 30 and 60 percent of the time.[27] In other words, a healthy amount of time looking away can avoid a feeling of incessant staring while still indicating a high level of interest.

In terms of eye contact during conversations with others, an excessive gaze has been linked to higher degrees of deceitfulness and lying. Theoretically, researchers suggest that the increased gaze is associated with the need for such individuals to assess nonverbal cues about the other person in an effort to manipulate them in some way.[28] At the same time, reduced eye contact can trigger the same impressions. A person with shifty eyes, who has difficulty making and sustaining eye contact, often comes across as dishonest at worst and poorly

---

27 Vanessa Martinez, "Lying Eyes, Or Something Else? How Blink Rate, Pupil Dilation Give Insight to Honesty and Attraction," *Medical Daily,* 2015, retrieved from http://www.medicaldaily.com/lying-eyes-or-something-else-how-blink-rate-pupil-dilation-give-insight-honesty-and-319164.

28 Ibid.

confident at best. When you want to be most appealing, you should shoot for the middle when it comes to eye contact. Engage enough to highlight your level of intrigue but not so much that you come across like a stalker.

Of course, the degree of eye contact you have with someone you know is quite different from that with a stranger across the room. That sexy glance in your direction can take your breath away and cause your heart to skip a beat within an instant. In these situations, the brief meeting of the eyes can suggest intrigue while also sending a more provocative message. Combine this with a smile, and you are clearly signaling a higher level of interest. Interestingly, men tend to be more attracted to women who they think are interested in them.[29] With a quick glance, you can easily convey your interest and potentially increase your allure at the same time.

We have already discussed the importance of highlighting the appearance of your eyes. Larger pupils, wider eyes, and lush eyelashes all enhance a youthful appearance and heightened reproductive potential. At the same time, sexy behaviors can further augment these beautiful features. Coming back again to Audrey Hepburn, she was known to enhance her eyelashes by using mascara and then separating each individual lash using a safety pin.[30] Why? By having pronounced eyelashes, she was able to draw greater attention to her eyes, and from there…well, she could captivate nearly any man on the planet.

---

29 De Deus, 2009.

30 Yagana Shah, "10 Vintage Beauty Secrets from Old Hollywood's Most Glamorous Stars," Huffington Post, 2015, retrieved from https://www.huffingtonpost.com/2015/03/27/vintage-beauty-secrets-old-hollywood-stars_n_6910752.html.

Our attention is automatically attracted to moving objects. When something in our view suddenly moves, we are hardwired to direct our gaze in that direction. By blinking and batting your eyelashes, you naturally highlight the appearance of your eyes. While this certainly relates to the appearance of beauty, the actual blinking of your eyes is also a behavior that enhances your level of attractiveness. Batting your eyelashes, like an attentive gaze, can signal a certain level of interest and intrigue that is often perceived as being quite attractive by others. At the same time, blinking too fast or rarely blinking can have the opposite effect.

So, how often should you blink? Again, science is here to help. Studies have demonstrated that blinking ten times a minute or more is associated with increased attractiveness. A lower frequency of blinking can evoke some level of mistrust. Many theorize that this perception of mistrust comes from the notion that you are too attentive for reasons other than a genuine interest.[31] At the same time, excessive blinking may come across as being nervous, inattentive, or a poorly confident. Thus, like Goldilocks, you want to be somewhere between these extremes to enhance your level of attractiveness.

You will not likely count the number of blinks per minute you have on a regular basis (nor should you). But appreciating that the use of your eyelashes and the frequency with which you blink are influential behaviors in promoting attractiveness is important. The same can be said about those brief, provocative glances and the amount of eye contact you have with others. In both cases, the goal is to express

31 Martinez, 2015.

the level of interest you have in a subtle yet sensual way. When you accomplish this objective, others will naturally perceive you to be more appealing, and your true beauty will be able to shine through.

Laughing and Smiling All the Way

> *"Keep smiling because life's a beautiful thing and there is so much to smile about"* **Marilyn Monroe**[32]

When it comes to attractive behaviors and those that enhance your beauty, smiling ranks at the top of the list. It may seem hard to believe, but smiling increases your sex appeal even more than wearing makeup. A study that surveyed over one thousand people found that over two-thirds ranked photographs of women who were smiling and had no makeup as more attractive than women who wore makeup but were not smiling.[33] That is certainly a pearl of wisdom that is good to know next time you have to leave the house in a rush.

This study is not the only evidence supporting the powerful effect smiling has on beauty. Other researchers examined a variety of different smiles across large populations and found all types of smiles correlated with higher levels of attractiveness (except for those that had a significant gap between their two front teeth). In fact, smiling correlated with attractiveness more than the appearance of women's eyes, hair, or facial features.[34] And still other research has found

32 Dave Farnham, *Snippets of Marilyn Monroe*, Dave Farnham Publishing, 2014.
33 Wrigley.com. "Face facts: Smiles more attractive than make-up," Wrigley.com, 2012, retrieved from http://www.wrigley.com/uk/press/news-details.aspx?id=1382.
34 De Deus, 2009.

that smiling can overcome other facial characteristics that might be considered less than appealing when measuring attractiveness.[35] All of these facts highlight the importance of smiling when you are unleashing your personal best.

Of course, not all smiles are equally attractive. Some smiles are more appealing than others, which relates back to their overall appearance. White, healthy teeth and a symmetric smile is typically seen as more attractive overall, and sometimes smiles that show too much of the gums are often associated with lower levels of attractiveness.[36] But even in these instances, smiling is better than not smiling. When we smile, we are seen as being happy, satisfied, and enjoying life. And more importantly, a smile signals to others we are happy to be in their presence and have a natural interest in them. Who wouldn't be attracted to someone like that? Many of the *Seven Days to Sexy* beauty tips will provide great insights into having the most beautiful smile possible, but you should also know that simply having a smile on your face goes a long way in increasing your sex appeal to others.

A sexy smile brightens your face and shows your ability to see things in a positive way. Let's face it…life can wear one down over time, and a beautiful smile implies a youthful demeanor that remains filled with joy, curiosity, and wonder. Because these attributes are associated with youthfulness, they are naturally attractive. In the same way, laughter can cause you to be more appealing and desirable to others. Of course,

---

35 Jessika Golle, Fred W. Mast, and Janek S. Lobmaier, "Something to smile about: The interrelationship between attractiveness and emotional expression," *Cognition & Emotion* 28, no. 2 (2014): 298–310.

36 Ibid.

we all want to be surrounded by positive, happy people, but laughter is more than simply an optimistic outlook. Laughter is a flirtatious way of telling someone they bring you joy, and this increases your level of attractiveness to them.

> *"To me, what's sexy is when you look like you're having a good time. That, and when you look effortless and have messy hair."* **Kate Upton** [37]

While laughter offers a compliment to others, laughter is also linked to youthfulness. In the film *Peggy Sue Gets Married*, Kathleen Turner plays the role of a middle-aged woman as well as a younger version of herself when she is suddenly transported back in time several decades to her high school days. In playing both age roles, Turner adopted a more youthful and flirtatious behavior when she needed to fit in with her teenage friends. How did she do this? She was more animated, had higher levels of energy, had a higher-pitched voice, and tended to giggle and laugh a lot more than when she was her middle-aged self. Like a pleasant smile, that youthful giggle can go a long way in making you more appealing.

While laughter and unsolicited smiles may be more common in youth, this is not the only time these behaviors seem to occur with greater regularity. Did you know that flirting behaviors are more common when women are in their ovulatory phase of their menstrual

---

37 Joyce Chen, "Kate Upton flaunts her cleavage, dons Daisy Dukes for Cosmopolitan: 'What's sexy is when you look like you're having a good time.'" *New York Daily Post*, 2012, retrieved from http://www.nydailynews.com/entertainment/gossip/kate-upton-flaunts-cleavage-dons-daisy-dukes-cosmo-article-1.1172858.

cycle? It's true! Studies have shown women tend to be more "flirty" around this time, and men tend to tip lap dancers greater amounts during a dancer's ovulation times as well. The behaviors that tend to increase during ovulation include both smiling and laughing as well as greater eye contact.[38] It would thus appear that smiles and laughter mean more than just youth...they also signal a higher chance of reproductive potential.

You now appreciate how (and why) smiling and laughing can enhance your beauty and allure. However, you may not be aware that the sound of your voice can do the same. Did you know that a higher tone or pitch in your voice has also been linked to higher levels of attractiveness? We are all familiar with the instant desire a sultry and sexy-sounding voice can trigger. In fact, a classic *Seinfeld* episode depicts this very concept when Elaine (Julia Louis-Dreyfus) secretly records a whispery, sexy voice onto Jerry's voice mail.[39] But while this may be the stereotype, men are actually more attracted to higher voice frequencies, according to large surveys.[40]

Higher voice frequencies are associated with youthfulness. Women also tend to have higher-pitched voices during ovulation.[41] Thus, like laughing and smiling, a higher voice tends to create higher appeal and desire among most men, presumably because these features are linked to better partner selection. In addition, everyone tends to climb

38 Stephanie M. Cantú, Jeffry A. Simpson, Vladas Griskevicius, Yanna J. Weisberg, Kristina M. Durante, and Daniel J. Beal, "Fertile and selectively flirty: Women's behavior toward men changes across the ovulatory cycle," *Psychological Science* 25, no. 2 (2014): 431–438.
39 David Steinberg (Director).,"The Tape," *Seinfeld,* Season 3, Episode 8, 1991.
40 Sarah A. Collins and Caroline Missing, "Vocal and visual attractiveness are related in women," *Animal Behaviour* 65, no. 5 (2003): 997–1004.
41 Cantu, 2014.

up an octave when they are excited and highly interested. When you do this, you naturally show your enthusiasm and energy level, which in turn also makes you more appealing. None of these little behavioral nuances are required for you to look sexy or beautiful, but each of them can help you raise the bar when it comes to appearing attractive to others.

Letting Your Body Do the Talking

In the words of the late, great Mae West, "I speak two languages...Body and English."[42] The sultry entertainer with an unashamed passion for men knew how to communicate her sexiness in a number of ways, but by far, she certainly was an expert in moving her physique in a way that made men drool. She inspired great art pieces by the infamous Salvador Dali, and servicemen even named an inflatable life vest after her in homage to her buxom figure.[43] Mae West was beautiful and sexy, and she could melt men's heart without saying a single word.

How you move and the body posture you take can speak volumes about you. You've noticed it. Dozens of people may walk into a coffee shop or restaurant hardly attracting any attention at all. But then suddenly, someone walks in with the perfect sway, an air of confidence, and sensual mannerisms that demand your attention. Many times, this has been defined as an essential part of charisma... the ability to generate positive feelings in others while drawing them

42 N.A., "Mae West quotes," Brainyquotes.com, 2017, retrieved from https://www.brainyquote.com/quotes/quotes/m/maewest380320.html.

43 N.A., "Mae West, Hollywood's Sex Symbol, Dies," *Washington Post*, 1980, retrieved from https://www.washingtonpost.com/archive/local/1980/11/23/mae-west-hollywoods-sex-symbol-dies/21d91e47-e6af-466a-8d4f-58506de45a65/?utm_term=.fab45e775c6d.

closer to yourself. No matter how you want to describe it, how you use and move your body plays a significant role in the level of desire you generate in others.

So, where do we start? How should you move and what body posture makes you the most appealing? Before we get into specifics, two important techniques can give you a bit of an advantage when using body language to showcase your sexiness and beauty. The first is symmetry. Movements that are pleasantly symmetric are naturally pleasing to the eye (as opposed to a limp, for example). They tend to be more artistic in nature and aesthetically pleasing.[44] When we discussed beauty and facial appearance, symmetry was an important feature, as it tended to imply good health and strong genes. These attributes were subconsciously attractive and seen as appealing. Well, the same thing applies to body language. Those movements that highlight symmetry are naturally seen as more sensual, sexy, and attractive.

The second interesting tidbit about body movement and attractiveness is mimicry. This might sound a little strange, but the more we tend to mimic the movements and positions of those with whom we interact, the more appealing we become.[45] Why would this be? Are we so self-absorbed that we seek out others that are mirror images of ourselves? Not really. However, we do tend to find people who share similar beliefs, attitudes, interests, and opinions as inherently more attractive. Finding someone who moves and behaves like ourselves during conversation, for example, makes us feel in tune, or on the same wavelength. The

---

44 M. Bertamini, C. Byrne, & K. M. Bennett, "Attractiveness is influenced by the relationship between postures of the viewer and the viewed person," *i-Perception* 4, no. 3(2013), 170–179.
45 Ibid.

next time you really want to get someone's attention, remember to let your body do some of the talking.

Understanding these basic concepts of body language and physical attraction, we can now move onto some specifics. Consider how you walk, for example. When you think about a sexy gait, what comes to mind? Holding a strong posture, leading with your chest, swiveling your hips back and forth as your arms swing loosely at your sides. The classic sexy strut is well known to most women (and men). But what is it about this walk that drives men crazy? How does moving your body in this manner make them exclaim, "I've got to get to know her!"

Let's break your sexy walk down piece by piece. What does that strong posture suggest? With head held high and with chest forward, your body position communicates a high level of confidence. It suggests you have figured things out and know how to succeed. While this might be intimidating to some, most men find such an air of confidence highly attractive. Why wouldn't they? After all, success is an attractive feature in anyone, and exuding confidence as you walk across the room allows your beauty to be readily apparent. This type of body posture also allows you to highlight symmetry, which increases your appearance of youthfulness, health, and well-being.

What about the way you move your hips? According to Shakira, the hips don't lie. And indeed, they don't. Just like batting your eyelashes draws attention to the beauty of your eyes, swaying your pelvis as you walk does the same thing for your waist and hips. Men cannot help but notice these physical attributes when the movement of your hips are demanding the attention of their gaze. And once focused on this part of your physique, you have the opportunity to showcase your "sexy" with proper dimensions of a waist-to-hip ratio. In this way, your body language helps you attract attention to your most beautiful and sensual features.

> *"One moves more slowly in heels. Walking fast is neither sexy nor engaging. Nobody notices the people who race around. If you're walking in heels, you've got time. It's much more attractive."* **Christian Louboutin**[46]

This brings us to one of the most appealing articles of clothing that women and men both find sexy...high heels. What is it about high heels that are so universally appealing? Interestingly, several details. First, high heels inherently change the way a woman walks. They shorten the length of the stride, enhance the tilt of the pelvis, and reduce the perceived size of the foot. Each of these serve to create a gait that is perceived as more feminine in nature. In fact, studies have shown that men are more prone to help a woman in high heels than they are for those in regular height shoes. The higher the heel, the more likely they were to lend a hand.[47]

As we will discuss later in this book regarding how to "think sexy," embracing a certain degree of femininity is important when trying to increase a sense of desire. While confidence is an attractive attribute, balancing this mindset with some degree of vulnerability can further

46 Mariana Mariesse and Katie L. Connor, "Christian Louboutin: In His Shoes," MarieClaire.com, 2012, retrieved from https://www.marieclaire.com/celebrity/a6920/christian-louboutin-interview/.

47 Nicolas Guéguen, "High heels increase women's attractiveness," *Archives of Sexual Behavior* 44, no. 8 (2015): 2227–2235.

enhance your sex appeal. Marilyn Monroe understood this perfectly well. She could switch gears from privately discussing career strategies to publicly using her body language to portray a sense of vulnerability and weakness that men found endearing and appealing. In essence, high heels help accomplish this same balance, as do other nuances of body position and posture.

In general, a more open body position also invites higher perceived levels of attractiveness. For example, sitting with arms folded and legs crossed can send a message of resistance and defensiveness. In contrast, using arm gestures, relaxing the shoulders, and adopting a more open stance or seated position has the opposite effect. If you are truly interested in making a positive impression on someone, paying attention to your body's movements and position is important. Even leaning forward can signal you are interested in what the other person has to say, and this inherently increases your appeal.

The way you position your body in space has a significant impact on how others will perceive you. Positioning yourself too far away from someone when speaking can give an impression of being disinterested or in a hurry to leave, and being too close can be a bit unnerving for the other person. The key is to be close enough to someone to show them that they have your full attention without invading their personal space. Combine this with some flirtatious behaviors, and you will be amazed at the influence this can have on their reaction to you.

A word should also be said about the use of touch in achieving greater allure and desire. Twirling the ends of your hair or slowly tucking the strands behind your ear is one way to appear more playful and seductive. Stroking the stem of your wine glass or fondling your jewelry can signal your desire to caress or be caressed. And lightly touching his arm or chest in a teasing manner can usually get his attention fairly quickly. While all these behaviors serve to perhaps express your own desire, they also make you appear more youthful, energetic, and interested...and each of these tend to come across as being sexier.

The way you use your body can have a profound effect on your level of sensuality and sex appeal. In fact, while teasing and poking fun at someone offers a more verbal level of flirting, the behaviors described in this chapter are generally recognized as effective in enhancing your attractiveness and allure. A smile, a pleasant laugh, a sexy strut, and an engaging body posture all serve as flirtatious behavioral extensions as does the use of touch. These techniques can be used to highlight your most attractive assets and enhance your natural beauty.

Chapter 3

The Power of Thinking Sexy

"I can flip on a switch in my brain, and even if the next Brad Pitt is sitting next to me, I won't look at him. But I can also turn that switch off, and then I collect attractive boys."
Megan Fox[48]

Do you remember the last time you felt attractive and sexy? Perhaps you had just stepped out for the evening, wearing those new Prada stilettos while strutting down the street. It might have been related to a variety of factors, but one thing is for certain...your self-confidence in the way you looked was at a record high. If only you could capture that feeling whenever you wanted. Wouldn't that be great? As a matter of fact, you can. All it takes is some key insights about how to adopt that sexy mindset on demand for any situation you like.

You now know what it takes to look sexy, and you also now appreciate many specific behaviors that enhance your attractiveness. But if you really want to embrace your sexiest and hottest self, having a mindset that ties all these things together can raise the bar exponentially.

48 Debrolina Raja, "What Causes Low Libido and Sexual Drive in Women?" HotFridayTalks.com, 2018, retrieved from https://www.hotfridaytalks.com/health/what-causes-low-libido-and-sexual-drive-in-women/attachment/megan-fox-500x360/.

Why is a sexy mindset important? Simply because synchronicity is the key when you want to be attractive and beautiful. Looking and acting the part is essential, but when combined with a frame of mind that oozes authentic and unapologetic confidence, your true beauty really shines through.

> *"I fall asleep feeling beautiful. Then, in the morning, before I leave the house, I say five things I love about myself, like 'You have pretty eyes.' That way I can go out into the world with that little bit of extra confidence. It's a feel-good protein shake in the back pocket in case someone messes with me that day."* **Jennifer Love Hewitt**[49]

In this chapter, you will learn several techniques and strategies to help you get your mind and mood aligned with the rest of your sexy self. This starts by looking within to see how you may feel about certain physical features and qualities unique to you. Identifying those little things that consciously or subconsciously bother you helps you know where to focus your attention. In addition, we'll discuss key tips about how to enhance confidence in your appearance through your clothes and self-care. And we'll also include a few activities that help prepare you mentally for that romantic encounter. Do you want to be your most beautiful and sexy self? Then, thinking sexy is another essential factor to consider.

---

49 *Shape Magazine*, "What makes celebs feel sexy," n.d., retrieved from https://www.shape.com/celebrities/celebrity-photos/what-makes-celebs-feel-sexythi.

What's Holding You Back?

> *"The implication is that to be sexual is to be trashy because being sexy means playing into men's desires. To me, 'sexy' is a kind of beauty, a kind of self-expression, one that is to be celebrated, one that is wonderfully female. Why does the implication have to be that sex is a thing men get to take from women and women give up?...Where can girls look to see women who find empowerment in deciding when and how to be or feel sexual? Even if being sexualized by society's gaze is demeaning, there must be a space where women can still be sexual when they choose to be."* **Emily Ratajkowski**[50]

When it comes to self-confidence about your appearance, you likely feel rather great about some things and less so about others. Perhaps you have always loved your long, slender and toned legs but are completely unsatisfied with the overall shape of your body. Maybe you have a beautiful face with naturally high cheekbones, but you are not pleased with the shape and size of your lips. All of us experience these emotions and opinions when we look in the mirror...me, you, Victoria Secret supermodels...everyone. Don't worry, you're in good company!

So, what does this have to do with having a sexy mindset? Everything! Whether you realize it or not, every time you think about those little

---

50 Heather Saul, "Emily Ratajkowski addresses body-shaming and criticism for demonstrating her sexuality in empowering essay." Independent, 2016. Retrieved from https://www.independent.co.uk/news/people/emily-ratajkowski-pens-essay-on-right-to-demonstrate-her-sexuality-a6878986.html.

things you dislike about your appearance, you see yourself as slightly less appealing to others. The key is to figure out what those little things are that drive you crazy so you can invest your energy in changing them. In many instances, you can use quick and simple techniques to overcome these minor hindrances and boost your self-confidence about your appearance immediately. Life's too short to let these minor imperfections hold you back from feeling sexy and beautiful.

When considering the effect your appearance has on your own mindset, you might be surprised at the magnitude of the impact. Research has explored this relationship and found high correlations between perceived attractiveness and a healthy mind. In one study that followed over ten thousand adults from their teenage years through middle age, researchers found that those who saw themselves as attractive had much higher levels of psychological wellness. Specifically, perceived facial attractiveness, ideal weight, and preferred height enhanced several psychological areas, including independence, confidence, relationships, and self-worth when compared to those who lacked positive self-perceptions.[51] The bottom line...a good feeling about how you look naturally creates a positive mindset.

The link between your self-confidence and the view you have of your level of attractiveness has been well recognized for decades. In the 1970s, medical college surgeons in Georgia and Virginia performed cosmetic surgery on several incarcerated individuals in an effort to enhance their self-image and outlook on life. Surgeons chose those

51 Nabanita Datta Gupta, Nancy L. Etcoff, and Mads M. Jaeger, "Beauty in mind: The effects of physical attractiveness on psychological well-being and distress," *Journal of Happiness Studies* 17, no. 3 (2016): 1313–1325.

with facial and dental disfigurations. It was the surgeons' opinion that these operations would have reduced the number of crimes committed among the group if they had only been addressed earlier.[52] While this study does not mean to suggest poor self-perceptions about attractiveness leads to crime, it does show how these self-perceptions can affect confidence. This supports the importance of identifying those things you see as less attractive so you can do something about them.

Let's take a more practical (and entertaining) example. Most everyone appreciates the star power that Dolly Parton has had for decades. In addition to her incredible voice, she is well recognized for her inherent beauty and her well-endowed physical attributes (which she readily acknowledges as one of her most proud investments). Dolly understands the impact that physical appearance has on one's frame of mind. In interviews, she has commented, "If I see something saggin', baggin', or draggin', I'm gonna have it nipped, tucked, or sucked!"[53] And even in her seventies, she continues to use fillers and Botox to look the best she can. Why? Because how she looks affects how she feels...and she likes to feel attractive.

Dolly Parton is an extroverted example of someone who owns up to the fact that she has had various procedures performed to enhance her appearance. In actuality, however, many celebrities regularly have beauty treatments and procedures but do not discuss them openly; some even deny them outright. These women are not overdone in

---

52 Donald B Egolf and Sondra L. Chester, *The Nonverbal Factor: Exploring the Other Side of Communication*, iUniverse, 2013.

53 Anne Brenoff, "6 things you may not know about Dolly Parton, on her 70th birthday," Huffington Post, 2016, retrieved from https://www.huffingtonpost.com/entry/6-things-you-may-not-know-about-dolly-parton-on-her-70th-bday_us_569cfbfae4b0b4eb759f100c.

their looks, and because the work they have had performed is artful, subtle, and consistent, it is not obvious to most people. This kind of restorative approach to beauty has prolonged the careers of many actresses, models, and musicians, whose careers in the past would have ended when they were thirty-five to forty years of age.

Of course, not every little imperfection requires attention. Which strategies you choose to consider, and which things you choose to address, are completely up to you. But to decide which steps to take, you first must identify those features that undermine your self-confidence and make you feel less attractive. Once you have done this, you will be able to better assess what strategies might work for you in helping you have that sexy mindset whenever you would like.

The desire to act to adjust specific physical features that tend to hold you back is a step toward empowerment. It is a way to still be yourself while striving to be a better you. However, it is not a remedy for someone who simply hates everything about themselves. Instead, it is a strategy that should be used to boost your confidence by addressing the little things that tend to bother you. Whether these little things include acne breakouts, scars, or an unsightly mole, addressing such features that inhibit you allows you to be your most confident.

Beauty Strategies for That Sexy Mindset

> *"The most alluring thing a woman can have is confidence. You can be beautiful, but if you're not secure in yourself, you don't come across as sexy. You have to feel good about*

yourself to make others feel good about you. Don't focus on the bits you don't like. Look at yourself in a different way and work out what it is you do like." **Beyoncé**[54]

Having defined those pesky things that drive you crazy and undermine your self-confidence, the next step involves doing something about it. Not every little flaw and defect requires aggressive measures. In fact, many simple and easy techniques can be used to overcome those barriers that keep you from feeling your sexiest and most beautiful. From dressing strategies to keeping up with some basic grooming procedures, you can adopt many practices that are guaranteed to help you get your sexy on.

To begin with, let's talk about the choices you make about what you wear. You have heard the term "dress for success," but have you ever considered what it truly means? At a basic level, it refers to dressing for the situation at hand. But on a deeper level, dressing for success reflects the need to look and feel that you can achieve anything you set out to do. In other words, the way you dress affects how you think about your abilities and opportunities. Nothing could be truer when it comes to thinking sexy.

When you consider the psychology behind fashion and how you dress, the clothes you wear should highlight your most attractive features. As discussed previously, some attributes are universally found to be more attractive than others. Using fashion to showcase these alluring attributes goes a long way in making you feel beautiful.

---

54 *Shape Magazine*, "What makes celebrities feel sexy," n.d., retrieved from https://www.shape.com/celebrities/celebrity-photos/what-makes-celebs-feel-sexy.

Purposefully choosing a fit, a style, and accessories that make heads turn will naturally make you feel sexy and appealing to others. The immediate feedback you receive when others compliment you about your look and appearance will automatically boost your confidence and ego.

> *"I'm a big fan of glamour. I enjoy putting on a sexy dress and heels. I want to work it."* **Ali Larter**[55]

The first rule of thumb is to choose clothing that highlights those features known to attract others' attention. For example, choosing an outfit that makes your waist appear smaller than your hips is typically more attractive. As previously discussed, a waist-to-hip ratio of 0.7 is ideal, and clothes that give this appearance can make you naturally look sexier.[56] However, the focus should be on shrinking the waist with your apparel as opposed to enlarging the look of your hips. Having a sleek look that continues to highlight your body's natural curves often helps achieve this appearance. And knowing this fact will inherently make you feel more confident and beautiful.

Tight-fitting clothes can also help showcase your natural feminine curves, but at the same time, your clothes should not be overly tight or small. Remember, moving with confidence is important when projecting your sexiest self. Uncomfortable clothing may make you

---

55 Molly Fahner, "Fun Fearless Female of the Year: Ali Larter," *Cosmopolitan Magazine*, 2009, retrieved from https://www.cosmopolitan.com/entertainment/celebs/news/a2783/ali-larter-cover-interview/.

56 Mohammad Atari, Razieh Chegeni, and Ladan Fathi, "Women who are interested in cosmetic surgery want it all: The association between considering cosmetic surgery and women's mate preferences," *Adaptive Human Behavior and Physiology* 3, no. 1 (2017): 61–70.

move awkwardly and project the opposite image. Similarly, leaving something to the imagination is key. If you choose a tight-fitting dress, perhaps leave the skin of the arms or legs covered. If you want to expose your midriff, then a longer skirt might be more enticing and sensually appealing. In essence, you want to draw attention to your shapely figure, but at the same time, you don't want to give away too much. Nothing is quite as powerful as the mind when it comes to anticipating what has yet to be revealed. The imagination is quite profound in this regard.

In choosing what clothes to wear, you want to highlight your most attractive features while minimizing your least attractive ones. Celebrities certainly take this approach when they want to look and feel their best. According to celebrity stylist Jen Rade, you should choose one body part that you feel confident about and show it off. If it's your cleavage, then choose a shirt or dress with flowing lines that draws attention to this area of your body. At the same time, she recommends covering up other areas to help maintain the focus on your most appealing attributes.[57] Strategically dressing to stress the positives and minimize the negatives will help you foster that sexy attitude that will inevitably boost your confidence as well.

Another fashion strategy to enhance your sex appeal is the use of sensual highlights. For example, wearing clothes with lace borders can soften your look while also giving a "peek-a-boo" feel. The same can be said about choosing a sexy, sheer dress that reveals a bit of skin

57 Alexis Bennett, "The 59 best fashion tips of all time," *InStyle Magazine*, 2017, retrieved from http://www.instyle.com/fashion/50-best-fashion-tips-all-time.

underneath. Once again, these types of clothes drive the imagination wild with potential opportunities while showcasing a classy, elegant look. Even clothing that has draping lines that lead the eye to those more sensual parts of your body offers the chance to get someone's undivided attention. How you choose to use these highlights is up to you, but they can often create a sense of beauty, sensuality, and softness that makes you feel sexy.

> *"There is a shade of red for every woman."* **Audrey Hepburn**[58]

The color of your clothing is also an important consideration. In studies examining diverse cultures, the color red is universally linked to enhanced sexual attractiveness. Women consistently choose red when trying to look their hottest, and men routinely associate red with greater sex appeal.[59] That does not mean you shouldn't choose other colors to enhance your beauty, but when you want to look your hottest, red is it. This bold choice in color is naturally alluring to the eye, and when you want to make your biggest splash, you might want to give it a try.

Certainly, your selection in clothes and fashion can change the way you feel about yourself. The more stylish you look, the more your assets are highlighted and the less noticeable those concerning areas are, and the more empowered, sexy, and beautiful you will feel. But

---

58 Katie Berrington, "Audrey Hepburn's life lesson," *Miss Vogue*, 2015, retrieved from http://www.vogue.co.uk/gallery/audrey-hepburn-best-quotes.

59 Sharron J. Lennon, Alyssa Dana Adomaitis, Jayoung Koo, and Kim KP Johnson, "Dress and sex: a review of empirical research involving human participants and published in refereed journals," *Fashion and Textiles* 4, no. 1 (2017): 14.

other strategies can work to boost your self-esteem about your sex appeal as well. One of the most important is self-grooming. This can involve simple things like shaping your eyebrows, whitening your teeth, or the consistency with which you keep up with your personal landscaping. It can also include more detailed efforts like body waxing, laser therapies, and self-tanning. In any of these instances, grooming can play a powerful role in how sexy and attractive you feel.

From an evolutionary perspective, grooming serves two basic purposes. First, grooming is a functional behavior because it promotes cleanliness and the prevention of illness. But at the same time, grooming also has aesthetic value. When you pay attention to your overall hygiene and bodily appearance, you are essentially recognizing your self-worth. Some scientists suggest the act of gently touching yourself during these activities also serves to boost self-esteem and self-value.[60] In short, paying attention to the details of how you look naturally enhances your self-confidence about your appearance.

When you choose to spruce yourself up on a regular basis, you also receive visual feedback that you are progressively more and more attractive. Each time you look in the mirror, you see the fruits of your labor, and this also helps raise your self-esteem regarding your appearance. Even adding a fragrance can have a tremendous impact. In one research study, forty-eight men and women were found to have significantly higher self-esteem and perceptions about their looks

---

60 Francis McGlone, Susannah Walker, and Rochelle Ackerley, "Affective Touch and Human Grooming Behaviours: Feeling Good and Looking Good," In *Affective Touch and the Neurophysiology of CT Afferents* (New York: Springer, 2016), 265–282.

when they used a perfume or cologne.[61] When you smell appealing and have taken the time to care for your body, your confidence about your attractiveness to others shines.

Other self-care activities can also serve as effective strategies to make you feel more sexy and beautiful. Just as dressing stylishly and paying attention to personal hygiene helps you appreciate your most attractive features, so can exercise and physical fitness. Getting enough rest and sleep is also helpful in allowing you to feel your best. But one of the most important techniques to feel sexier involves overcoming negative self-talk. Overcoming that little voice inside your head that constantly points out the problem rather than the solution is essential when trying to think sexy.

As we will describe in the second part of this book, many ways to enhance your beauty and attractiveness are accessible to you that provide the means to look your absolute hottest. Understanding this, you can appreciate why critical thoughts in your head have little benefit other than highlighting areas that bother you the most. To overcome these hindrances, I suggest you use a "3-S" approach… smiling, socializing, and self-affirmations. Using this simple strategy, you can quickly shift your perspective from one of self-criticism to one of self-confidence.

By smiling, you choose to look on the positive instead of the negative, and smiles always provoke positive feedback from others. Smiling, even when intentional, is known to release endorphins and serotonin

61 J. Paasschen, Susannah C. Walker, Nicola Phillips, Paul E. Downing, and Steven P. Tipper, "The effect of personal grooming on self□perceived body image," *International Journal of Cosmetic Science* 37, no. 1 (2015): 108–115.

(happy hormones) in the brain. By socializing, you distract your mind and reduce the opportunity for negative thoughts to occur. And self-affirmations force you to see yourself in the most favorable way, calling attention to your most attractive and beautiful features. When combined with "success" dressing and dedicated self-care, these techniques provide powerful ways to realize your potential in being your sexiest self. Used together, these strategies allow you to have that sexy mindset while keeping you prepared for whatever might come your way.

Pre-Game Preparations to Psych You Up

> "*When I want to feel sexy, I like to dance—even if I'm at home by myself in my knee-high socks sliding there like* Risky Business...*my sisters and I, if one of us starts, we're all there in front of the mirror, dancing, and it's just obnoxious. I feel sexy when I do that.*" **AnnaLynne McCord**[62]

So, the big evening has arrived. You have planned your exact wardrobe, shoes, and jewelry for the occasion, and you have spent the week making sure your appearance is top-notch. You can feel your confidence and self-esteem begin to rise, but deep down, a slight sense of anxiousness exists. What if something goes wrong? What if you say or do the wrong thing? Maybe you are worried you forgot some small detail, or perhaps you continue to focus on some slight imperfection despite

62 *People Magazine*, "AnnaLynne McCord channels Tom Cruise to feel sexy," 2010, retrieved from http://people.com/celebrity/quoted-annalynne-mccord-channels-tom-cruise-to-feel-sexy/.

your efforts to minimize the negatives and accentuate the positives. In a word, it is called anxiety, and many women experience it before a social event or possible romantic encounter.

Believe it or not, anxiety can be a good thing. It's true. A little bit of anxiety is what motivates us to be proactive and prepare. It helps us look our most beautiful by discerningly choosing the right dress, cosmetics, shoes, and so on. However, too much of it can undermine how we feel about the way we look, and this hinders that sexy attitude in the process. Fortunately, several strategies can reduce the stress you may feel about your appearance while helping you reclaim that empowered sense of sensuality.[63] I call this the "pregame warmup" because it helps you have that sexy mindset that exudes confidence and self-esteem.

If we study various celebrities, we find they often use pregame rituals to help them feel confident about their appearance and abilities. For example, Ellen DeGeneres relies on transcendental meditation to help ease anxiety and to feel empowered.[64] Former Miss World, Priyanka Chopra, puts on her headphones and immerses herself in videos and music before a big event. And several find a rigorous exercise routine bolsters their confidence and makes them feel energized.[65] From meditation, to yoga, to music, to even dancing in front of the mirror,

---

63 Alison Wood Brooks, Juliana Schroeder, Jane L. Risen, Francesca Gino, Adam D. Galinsky, Michael I. Norton, and Maurice E. Schweitzer, "Don't stop believing: Rituals improve performance by decreasing anxiety," *Organizational Behavior and Human Decision Processes* 137 (2016): 71–85.

64 *Katherine*, "8 successful celebrities and their daily rituals," *The Richest*, 2014, retrieved from https://www.therichest.com/expensive-lifestyle/8-successful-celebrities-and-their-daily-rituals/.

65 Kaitlyn McLintock, "9 celebrities share their advice on how to feel confident," Byrdie.com, 2016, retrieved from http://www.byrdie.com/celebrity-confidence-tips.

many activities can help you adopt a more positive and confident mindset before facing the world. If it works for these celebrities and models, it can work for you as well.

> *"I feel the sexiest when I'm by myself, walking around nude. I have this new obsession with nudity, it's really weird. It may sound weird, but I just really love embracing the body."*
> **Ciara**[66]

One of the most effective ways to psych yourself up is through repeating positive self-affirmations. By focusing on those positive physical features that you know are alluring, you naturally distract your mind from anything negative. Similarly, visualizing success and an attitude of sex appeal furthers these efforts. You might even go so far as writing yourself love notes bragging about how awesome you look. You might even take the time to put a self-admiration next to some beautiful flowers that you give to yourself. You've probably heard about celebrities writing letters to their sixteen-year-old selves; why not write letters to yourself now? There is something about holding something tangible in your hands and seeing it in writing that can be quite powerful in boosting your morale.

As a final word, you may find that a cocktail or glass of wine may also do the trick when it comes to raising your self-esteem about your appearance. A few sips of chardonnay or a mini-cocktail will serve to appease your anxiety and, at the same time, provide a little

66 Leslie Pitterson, "Ciara talks baring it all," Clutch Magazine Online, n.d., retrieved from https://clutchmagonline.com/2011/05/ciara-talks-baring-it-all-when-do-feel-your-sexiest-glammed-up-or-dressed-down/.

bit of disinhibition. Of course, this would not be wise if driving to an event or restaurant, but in moderation, this too can help to make you drop some inhibition about your sexual appeal and attractiveness. Ultimately, whatever activities make you feel more confident and empowered about your looks should be part of your preparation ritual. This serves as the proverbial "cherry on top" and helps you pull out all the stops in being the hottest and sexiest self you can be.

Parting Thoughts and the Power of Possibility

> *"I just really want it at some point to be OK for women and young girls to be sexy because I think that's a power, a gift that we were given by God or the universe or whatever."*
> **Megan Fox**[67]

Possibility dressing is a term that alludes to your choice of clothing and even underclothing in hopes of a potential romantic encounter. After all, anything might happen at any time, right? Taking this idea a bit further, a possibility mindset can extend to include everything you do to make yourself the most beautiful you can be. Clothes, grooming, cosmetics, and even your undergarments all pertain to such a mindset, and by paying attention to all these areas, you enjoy the ability to pull out your sexiest attitude whenever you like.

Even though you may not expect a romantic encounter to occur, being prepared and at the top of your game can significantly affect

---

67 John Hiscock, "Megan Fox: interview for Jennifer's Body," Telegraph, 2009, retrieved from https://www.telegraph.co.uk/culture/film/6398707/Megan-Fox-interview-on-Jennifers-Body.html.

how you think about yourself. Knowing your lacey black lingerie, your low-cut sheer blouse, and your curvaceous red skirt make you look irresistibly appealing naturally boosts your confidence, as does your glowing skin, bright smile, and alluring perfume. Consistently paying attention to these things, even when you don't anticipate anything out of the ordinary, provides you with the confidence of knowing that you can always pull out your sexy when needed. Such pursuits can similarly enhance your existing relationships and add sauce to your romance as your level of self-assuredness increases.[68]

> "*Wear something saucy underneath your clothes, like risqué lingerie.*" **Carmen Electra**[69]

When you want to feel beautiful and sexy, pay special attention when choosing your undergarments. Have you ever worn a sexy bra that made you feel absolutely incredible despite the fact no one else could see it? Interestingly, research focus groups have shown that women tend to develop key aspects of their personality and persona by experimenting with different lingerie.[70] Even if hidden from view, your lingerie continues to have a powerful effect on your psyche and identity. Just knowing you are wearing something exquisitely sexy and enticing underneath can change your entire attitude and demeanor. And if somewhat revealed, the effect can be even more powerful. It's not always about how sexy you look to others…it's also about how

---

68 Alan Loy McGinnis, *The Romance Factor* (New York: HarperCollins, 1990).
69 *Cosmopolitan Magazine*, "The hot things celebs tell Cosmo," 2011, retrieved from https://www.cosmopolitan.com/entertainment/celebs/news/g1326/sexy-quotes-from-cosmo-cover-girls/.
70 Christiana Tsaousi and Joanna Brewis, "Are you feeling special today? Underwear and the 'fashioning 'of female identity." *Culture and Organization* 19, no. 1 (2013): 1–21.

sexy you feel. Sexy underwear is a perfect example of how you can adopt a sexier attitude simply by knowing a potential "fire" exists beneath the surface.

> *"I don't care what I'm wearing—if it's a frumpy T-shirt, sweats…if I still have a pair of pretty panties on, or a beautiful bra that makes me feel like a woman, those choices dictate the mood throughout the day."* **Brooke Burke**[71]

The power of possibility is another way you can enhance the way you feel and think when it comes to your sexual attractiveness and beauty. Just like the fashion you wear and the things you do to highlight your most attractive features, allowing yourself to be ready for the unexpected helps you embrace a sexy attitude when the need arises. A sexy attitude is one that is bold, confident, and assertive. It is one that exhibits passion and pursues pleasing desires. And it exudes a natural level of excitement and energy that others find irresistible. Utilizing all the beauty strategies highlighted in this chapter to gain such an attitude can be incredibly powerful and lets you truly be your most charismatic self.

So, what can you do to enlist the power of thinking sexy? A sexy attitude essentially reflects how you feel about yourself inside. In this regard, having that inner self-confidence and self-esteem is important, and accepting yourself and your unique beauty as special is similarly essential. But in addition, dressing for success further promotes

71 *Shape Magazine*, "What makes celebs feel sexy," n.d., retrieved from https://www.shape.com/celebrities/celebrity-photos/what-makes-celebs-feel-sexy.

confidence and self-esteem as does paying attention to personal grooming and always being prepared to "turn it on" when needed. Likewise, silencing negative perceptions and thoughts through mental strategies and empowering rituals can also serve you well. The way you look, act, *AND* think all work together to create a sensual and alluring persona that others will see as sexy, beautiful, and attractive. The whole is greater than the sum of these individual parts, and adopting a confident and positive attitude allows your beauty to shine that much more from every point of view.

PART II

Being Your Sexiest in Seven Days, Seven Weeks, Seven Months

Have you dreamt of looking like one of those dazzling celebrities sashaying down the red carpet or mesmerizing the crowd like a Victoria's Secret supermodel who emerges from a limousine? If you're like most women, I am sure you have. These gorgeous individuals demand everyone's gaze and radiate a sense of sex appeal that is awe-inspiring. You might have assumed that enjoying such a moment was out of your reach, but nothing could be further from the truth. Each of us can unleash our sexy if we so choose. The key is knowing how to go about it and being prepared to turn your sexy on when that special moment calls for it. Justin Timberlake knew what he was talking about when he said he was bringing sexy back.

Over the course of my professional career, I have learned dozens of techniques that are certain to bring out your most beautiful self. You might have wondered, "How can her legs look so toned and her skin so smooth and silky all the time?" Or you might have been amazed at how ageless these celebrities and models seem to be year after year. Trust me, all these women have little tricks up their sleeve to create their perpetually glamorous look whenever the public or paparazzi are around. The good news is that I can share those little tricks and beauty tips with you. By picking and choosing which beauty techniques you want to pursue, you can similarly unleash your own sexy style just like those who you have always admired.

In the preceding section, we have discussed how you can be your sexiest and why specific looks, behaviors, and attitudes create that irresistible attractiveness others cannot help but notice. Now, it is time to put those strategies into practice. In the chapters to follow, you will learn specific techniques and strategies that you can do to achieve your utmost beauty and appeal. Whether you want to boost your sex appeal in a matter of days or weeks, or whether you are committed to a more long-term approach to enhancing your appearance, an array of different beauty tips and practices can help you achieve just that. Want to be your sexiest? Of course, you do. So, let's get started…it's time to be that sexy, captivating, irresistible beauty you have always wished you could be.

Chapter 4

Seven Days to Sexy

It's Monday morning, and you are still wishing that the weekend had never come to an end, especially this particular Monday. While the beginning of the week often carries a bit of melancholy, the feeling is a little heavier than normal. Why? Because you met that special someone over the weekend who you can hardly quit thinking about. But there is a silver lining...he asked to see you again the upcoming weekend. In just seven days, you will have the chance to see him again. But wait...that is only seven days away. OMG! You only have a week to prepare and to make that spectacular impression on him that you want to make. Never fear...*Seven Days to Sexy* is here!

You might have a hot date coming up next weekend, or you might have a gala reunion affair where you want to look your absolute best. Regardless of the occasion, several beauty tips can make you look your best in just seven short days. The following day-by-day guide provides you with a recipe for achieving the look perfect for that special night out. Depending on your personal preferences, you can pick and choose activities that best suit your needs. You can select only a few, or you can pull out all the stops. Either way, the beauty tips provided offer you a stepwise approach to being ready to be your sexiest self in no time.

Seven Days to Sexy – Day 1: Appointments and Procedures

> *"Every woman should try a Brazilian wax once. And then the sex they have afterward will make them keep coming back!"* **Eva Longoria**[72]

Let's get started. Luckily, there are many procedures for the face that heal in exactly seven days. For Day 1, you will want to accomplish two major things: First, you will want to make appointments for certain activities for later in the week to ensure you have time and availability to accomplish all you wish to complete before the big day. And second, you will want to have all those procedures done that might take a few days from which to recover. In doing so, you will free up the rest of the week for putting on the finishing touches that allow you to look your absolute best.

Regarding scheduling appointments, if you will be wanting to do certain enhancing activities that require the assistance of a professional, you'll want to schedule these for early in the week. Ideally, I recommend you consult with a dermatologist for these procedures for them to be performed well and to address any questions and concerns you may have. For this reason, these appointments should preferentially be done the first day of your seven days to sexy so you have enough time to

72 Jennifer Graham, "All about Eva." *Cosmopolitan Magazine*, 2005, retrieved from https://www.cosmopolitan.com/entertainment/celebs/news/a1637/all-about-eva/.

heal. If you already have been seeing such a professional, then having them complete these procedures will be easy. But if not, seeing the right professional as soon as you can is certainly encouraged.

If you are considering any procedures from the following list, you will want to schedule appointments for them on Day 1 so all the beauty tips you have selected can be successfully completed before the week's end.

- *Dermatology Appointment* – Ideally this should be arranged on Day 1 or as soon as possible so that various procedures, if needed or desired, can be performed earlier in the week rather than later. The specific procedures included in a dermatology appointment for Day 1 will be identified in detail in the second part of Day 1's activities.
- *Hair Stylist Appointment* – Depending on the time of year and season, getting in to see your hair stylist can be challenging. Therefore, make the appointment on Day 1 to ensure availability later in the week, preferably on the day of your special occasion.
- *Body Waxing Appointment* – Like hair stylist appointments, body waxing appointments may also be difficult to arrange last minute. Call on Day 1 to schedule a waxing appointment for sometime during the week.
- *Pedicure and Manicure Appointment* – Make sure you have time and the chance to pop into the nail salon later in the week since these procedures naturally polish up and enhance your look.
- *Cosmetic Consultant Appointment* – You can always learn something new when it comes to cosmetics. Whether it involves

a makeover or simply the opportunity to learn about some of the latest and greatest tricks related to cosmetics, consider making such an appointment during the week at the Chanel or MAC counter to help develop the look you are going for and buy the makeup you may need.

- *Tanning Appointment* – If you choose a more professional approach to self-tanning, also use Day 1 to arrange a sunless tanning appointment for later in the week. You can alternatively buy products to use at home instead.

In addition to scheduling appointments, the following procedures and activities should be performed or started on Day 1 in order to have time to recover and receive the most benefit from these activities.

- *Dieting and Nutrition* – Wanting to lose a few pounds or give an added boost to your appearance is certainly not uncommon before a big event approaches. One way you can help achieve these goals is through healthy dieting and meal planning. If losing a bit around your waist and hips is the goal, try reducing your carbohydrates (breads, pasta, cereals, cheese etc.) and increasing the amount of proteins and fiber (select fruits, vegetables, high-fiber grains, and lean meats). One thing you will not want to do is restrict your fluid intake or take diuretic pills. These activities (along with caffeinated beverages) are naturally dehydrating, which can make your skin look less healthy and attractive than it otherwise might. Instead, drink ample water and supplement with vitamins to ensure that healthy glow. We will discuss which diet I prefer in the seven weeks and seven months to sexy chapter. Here, time is of the essence, so we will discuss doing our best with little time.

- *GI Cleanse* – In sticking with the theme of inside out, preparing to be your most attractive may also include a GI cleanse or detoxification. Over time, various unhealthy food substances enter our bodies, and helping our bodies rid themselves of this buildup reduces excess bloating and helps our body function at its best. This means your skin has a healthier glow, you have higher levels of energy, and you allow your body to take on its more naturally healthy shape. Most cleansing diets involve eating an abundance of fresh vegetables, citrus fruits, nuts, and high antioxidant foodstuffs while eliminating refined sugars, processed foods, high fat content items, and foods containing potentially allergenic ingredients like gluten. Many last seven to fourteen days, but some effective three-day cleansing diets are also available. Suja Juice® and Raw® are two companies that make premade juice cleanse products available on Amazon.com. The idea of the cleanse is to shrink the stomach, reduce bloating in the intestinal tract, and make you feel your best. You should stay hydrated during this time and end your cleanse well before your event/date so you are not weak and lightheaded. The point is to feel your best by Day 7.
- *Exercise and Fitness* – Another great strategy to boost your confidence, shed some extra water weight, *AND* suppress your appetite is to invest in some daily exercise and physical activities.

You don't have to go crazy here. Simply make some time to go to the gym consistently and push a little harder. A little can go a long way, and you should not overdo it the week before a special occasion. You don't want to be too sore or tired to be your very best. Remember you might need to rock those heels, and you need to be poised—not limping.

- *Corset Training* – This technique to enhance the hourglass figure and achieve that ideal waist-to-hip ratio has been around for centuries in various cultures, but most recently, celebrities like Kim Kardashian have promoted this technique to enhance body shape. Corset training can be used as part of your exercise routine or simply as part of your daily wear. The effects of reshaping your curves are semi-permanent, but it does take time to take effect. Starting on Day 1 will help you see some positive effects by the end of the week, and continued use will permit ongoing benefits. In terms of specific guidance with corset use, it should fit snugly without bulges but not interfere with breathing or cause pain. Likewise, over time, tightening adjustments are needed, but this may not be the case during the first seven days. Corset training is safest when done in the reclining (evening relaxation time) or lying down position (bedtime) for about three hours per day. I do not recommend corset training during long periods of standing or during strenuous exercise. Ann Chery® makes waist training corsets of all sizes and shapes—all of them sexy and available on Annchery.com as well as Amazon.com for convenience.

- *Facial Peels* – Looking for a quick way to make the skin look more youthful and toned? Superficial facial peels offer one technique that might be used in this regard. Facial peels involve the application of a mild chemical to the skin of the face that results in a light flush. Subsequently, the top layer of skin "peels" away, leaving smoother, more youthful-looking skin. Facial peels can be used to reduce wrinkles, prior skin sun damage, aging effects, and various types of pigmented skin lesions. In order to be ready in seven days, the peel must be administered by an experienced practitioner. My favorite low-down-time peel is the Jessner's peel. While mild facial peels are done flaking within seven days, moderate peels that involve greater depths of the skin can take up to fourteen days to peel and heal. You must communicate with your doctor to choose the type of facial procedure that has a healing time that correlates with the event you will be attending.
- *Ultherapy®* – This beauty enhancing procedure reaches a much deeper level than peels, and addresses different concerns. It is noninvasive and involves the use of ultrasound rather than topical solutions. In addition, its effects occur deeper in the skin in the dermal layers (roughly 5 mm depth) to stimulate collagen contraction (tightening) and new collagen formation rather than removing layers of skin. With time and hormonal changes, women tend to have a decline in their amount of collagen, which is what provides plump, smooth-appearing skin that does not ripple with facial expression. Therefore, by

stimulating collagen formation, Ultherapy helps lift and tighten the skin where treated. Ultherapy is administered to treat such issues as lifting brows, firming jowls, and tightening the skin on the neck. While the full effect may take three to six months, benefits from Ultherapy can be seen as early as the day of treatment. Discuss this procedure with your dermatologist to determine whether it is right for you. It can be combined on the same day with a light peel, as it addresses skin laxity (looseness) concerns rather than surface pigment and lines.

- *ScarLet SRF®* – ScarLet SRF is a recent, FDA-approved technology that is designed to tighten, smooth, and rejuvenate collagen. It uses a radiofrequency microneedling device to deliver energy to the underside of the skin. With minimal discomfort, this procedure provides surprising results in the rejuvenation arena. This device was first approved in Korea with an excellent safety record. Radiofrequency delivered to the dermis, or "hide" of the skin, causes it to contract, resulting in an immediate tightening effect. This clinical dose of energy also induces a healing response that promotes new collagen formation. It is the perfect combination of instant and long-term results. It is ideal for all skin types and helps firm the skin of the neck and jowls…even the whole face. Mild redness can be expected for up to twenty-four hours, which makes this procedure a perfect choice for those who have only seven days until the big event. It is also great for improving acne scars and reducing pore size. Currently, it is recommended as a series of three monthly treatments; however, this recommendation may change to a biannual schedule.

- *VBeam® Laser Therapy* – This beauty procedure has been around for several years now, and it is proven to be safe and effective for many skin conditions that affect appearance. Specifically, VBeam laser therapy can be used to reduce skin redness, rosacea, and broken blood vessels. It stimulates collagen, leaving the skin smoother than before—after a two-day healing process. With the Perfecta® attachment, the VBeam pulsed-dye laser also reduces age spots, sun spots, freckles, and other pigmented lesions with a seven-day healing period. In essence, the VBeam laser is pulsed at a targeted area at a single wavelength that contains specific color pigments included in blood vessels and red flushed areas. Why is this important? Because VBeam laser therapy reduces the appearance of unwanted veins and vascular lesions without damaging surrounding tissues. With the Perfecta attachment that focuses the laser beam to the skin's surface, it can also be used to change pigmented areas to better match your own skin tone. Although normally recommended as a series of three to eight treatments, it heals with visible improvement within a couple of days for a beneficial effect, which is ideal when you only have seven days before that important date.
- *Intense Pulsed Light (IPL) Therapy* – Unlike the VBeam, IPL is not a laser but is instead a high-intensity light that mimics multiple wavelengths of lasers when pulsed very close to the skin. Light wavelength filters are used to increase its specificity.

As a result, this beauty procedure can target precise superficial areas of the epidermis or be used in deeper dermal layers. This allows a more selective area to be treated without injury to other tissue areas. IPL is particularly good at safely and affordably lifting off age spots and sun-damaged skin areas. It is recommended as a series (four to six treatments) with the initial treatment showing the most improvement. Likewise, its recovery time is only seven days when done on the face.

- *A note about who should do your procedures*: There are many different devices that address similar skin concerns that we have mentioned. It is best to choose a board-certified dermatologist or plastic surgeon. The devices may vary, but the knowledge, skill, and experience of the physician team doing the procedures is most important. First, this ensures that the procedure chosen for your condition is the right one, and then of course, that it is done safely and properly. Smaller medi-spas have fewer devices and tend to take the "when you have a hammer, everything is a nail" approach. Their staff often undergoes frequent turnover, and therefore experience and training levels can be variable. Trust your skin to the best!

Seven Days to Sexy – Day 2: Lips and Eyes

"Never underestimate the power of red lipstick and high heels." **Unknown**

Nothing is as profoundly attractive as luscious lips and sexy eyes. Therefore, investing in these areas to enhance your beauty and sex appeal requires both time and energy. For Day 2, you will want to pursue activities that will serve to create that specific look of your lips and eyes that will make a tremendous splash when you walk in the room. The following are some excellent considerations to do just that.

- *Lip Fillers* – Luscious lips are full, shapely, and plump with rich color and moistness. If you want to attract attention, starting with the lips is an excellent idea. With lip filler injections, lips are everted to a greater extent and allow a fuller pout that is highly sensual and alluring. By injecting fillers like hyaluronic acid into the lip tissues, the lips have a more robust appearance that can last from nine to twelve months after an injection. The results are also immediate, although healing and maximum effect occur after a few days' waiting time. The lips do swell for two days after the procedure, and bruising is possible but preventable by using careful injector technique, maintaining pressure, and avoiding blood thinners such as aspirin and ibuprofen the week before. We also advise no alcohol the night before injections. If you are prone to cold sores, a dose or two of the medicine you normally take for that is recommended the night before and the day of.

- One of my favorite fillers for the lips is Juvéderm® or Juvéderm Volbella®, depending on the effect you would like to achieve. Natural-looking lip enhancement is possible and occurs daily—maybe hourly—in my office. The poor impression people get regarding lip injectables is from people they have seen who are completely overdone. Unfortunately, one bad lip job can deter thousands of people from every trying lip enhancement. Celebrities today, young and old, avail themselves of lip and cheekbone injections. Sometimes we fill the jawline and temples as well. My current favorite for these areas is Juvéderm® Voluma. Of course, these individuals have beautiful features anyway, but they take them from beautiful to bombshell with artfully performed injectables.
- *Lip Suctioning* – Although lip injections are not in everyone's budget, there are alternatives to enhance the appearance of the lips. While this does not have to be performed on Day 2, you might want to experiment with such techniques early in the week to determine how and if this might be a desirable approach to enhancing the appearance of your lips. These devices work by "sucking" blood flow and swelling into the lips, creating fuller, redder lips with an enhanced contour. After applying suctioning pressure for fifteen to thirty seconds at a time along your lips, this procedure is effective in creating a more alluring look, but at the same time, the effect lasts up to two hours only. Fullips®,

made popular by Kylie Jenner, is perhaps the most recognized brand of these devices. While lip suctioning can be effective in achieving the look you might desire quickly, application should be used infrequently to avoid tissue injury. As with everything else, this can be overdone, and young women have injured and bruised their lips attempting to look like Kylie. Please practice moderation. JuvaLips® is another product available at myjuvalips.com or Amazon.com.

- *Lip Plumping Gloss* – Similar to lip suctioning, lip gloss applications (used to "plump" the lips) do not have to be performed on Day 2, but you should experiment with such products ahead of time in order to test their effects and to determine how best to use them. In essence, these products work by filling the lips with tiny microphores that absorb fluid and enhance circulation to the lips, creating a fuller, plumper, and sexier look in the process. Soap & Glory's Sexy Mother Pucker® is a brand that fits our theme. Another effective brand is GrandeLIPS® Hydrating Lip Plumper, available at Sephora.com.
- *Neuromodulator Injections* – Neuromodulator toxin injections, aka Botox®, Dysport®, or Xeomin,® are examples of other highly effective procedures that can help eliminate and reduce unwanted wrinkles and to give the brows a bit of a lift. All the muscles of facial expression are in balance and somewhat in opposition of each other. By strategically relaxing the muscles of the face that pull downward and allowing the "lifters" to dominate, wrinkles are less pronounced, and areas such as the

lateral eyebrows and corners of the mouth can be lifted. This creates a much more youthful look. Again, when artfully and conservatively done, faces treated with Botox (i.e. 95 percent of Hollywood) look youthful and natural. It is the person who is overdone, shiny, and reptilian with brow peaks that are too high that keeps people from ever trying Botox. In truth, Botox prevents formation of deeper lines with time, by preventing repetitive expressions that imprint lines deeper in the dermis. I liken it to folding a piece of paper over and over in the same spot. The crease becomes deeper and deeper, and will be almost impossible to smooth out. Botox is relatively affordable and takes effect quickly, within three to seven days. There is a chance of bruising, so again we recommend avoidance of blood thinners such as aspirin and ibuprofen the week before treatment.

- When searching for a quote from someone who uses Botox, few if any celebrities are willing to admit they have had this procedure done. In my experience, however, it is a given rather than an exception among celebrities. Of course, this procedure must be performed in moderation to preserve some expression without the lines. The truth is, celebrities endure an unprecedented level of scrutiny, not only in their private lives, but everywhere. Cell phones are at the ready to snap selfies and photos of these individuals who are expected to look perfect at all times. The few that do admit to injectables see their career accomplishments, talent, and natural beauty marginalized as they are asked to discuss the fact that they've had injectable treatments. Soon, the big secret that is no secret will become mainstream, but for now the stigma, particularly for injectables, is in full force.

- *Eyelash Extensions* – Long, thick, dark eyelashes call attention to the eyes, and therefore, they naturally enhance your beauty and sexual allure. It is easy to underestimate the beauty of eyelashes, but when you think about it, every drawing of a beautiful princess includes long, gorgeous eyelashes. One effective way to achieve such a look is by using eyelash extensions, and the good news is that these do not cost a fortune or require a lot of time. Eyelash extensions are glued to your own lashes by a trained aesthetician, creating a longer look. They last two to three weeks and then need to be filled. The upside is beautiful lashes any time of the day and night, i.e., "I woke up like this," and the downside is that your natural lashes are damaged a bit when you get them removed—not permanently, of course, because they do grow back. Occasionally, people become allergic to the glue that is used to attach these individual lashes. You may alternately choose to apply lash strips yourself with Duo® glue (a different, temporary glue). This takes a bit of practice. I suggest you practice applying these with tweezers for a few days before your event unless you want to feel murderous just moments before your special date. My favorite brand of lash strips is Ardell®. They are flexible, comfortable, and affordable... and available at your local drugstore. A little trial and error will help you figure out which style and length fits you best.

- *Eyelash Treatments* – You may not be comfortable with anything attached to your eyelashes, and in that case, eyelash enhancers can be applied nightly to encourage the growth of your own lashes. These prostaglandin analogs create thicker, longer, and darker eyelashes. Latisse® prescription-strength eyelash enhancer has been approved since 2008 for this use. Its application can double your lash thickness while also slightly increasing length and richness of color. You simply apply the enhancer nightly for the first several months to the root of the upper eyelashes; the full effect is realized several weeks later. In addition to mascara and other eyelash enhancers, these eyelash treatments significantly augment the attractiveness of your eyes. These topical treatments also enhance eyebrow hair growth and can ameliorate gaps in the brows. My favorite over-the-counter options are GrandeLash® and GrandeBROW® products, available at Sephora.com.

Seven Days to Sexy – Day 3: Shopping!

> *"A woman's dress should be like a barbed-wire fence: serving its purpose without obstructing the view."* **Sophia Loren**[73]

After two full days of making appointments and completing beauty procedures, it's time to have some fun…let's go shopping. You definitely

73 Katherine Hutchinson-Hayes, PhD, *God's Little Black Dress for Women: How to Put on the Full Armor of God Without Losing Your Femininity*, Lulu.com, 2012.

don't want to wait until the last minute to scramble for something to wear for the big occasion. Strategically choose those items that will accentuate your beauty and attractiveness in advance. In doing so, when the day arrives, concerns about what to wear won't add to your worries or interfere with your confidence. And definitely enjoy yourself while shopping!

> *"Don't be into trends. Don't make fashion own you, but you decide what you are, what you want to express by the way you dress and the way you live."* **Gianni Versace**[74]

- *The Perfect Outfit* – As previously discussed, you will want to closely consider many factors when choosing what you will wear for a special occasion where you want to look your most attractive and beautiful. First, you must consider the style of dress appropriate for the event. Likewise, you need to select clothing that highlights your most attractive features, optimizes your waist-to-hip ratio, and creates a sense of wonder for the imagination. Sexy accents, strategic reveals, and enticing colors are all areas that deserve your attention. Take your time and choose wisely. And if needed, enlist the services of a couture specialist or fashion-savvy friend. Having the right attire can pull everything together in a way that will significantly enhance your beauty and sex appeal.

74 Daisy Fuentes, *Unforgettable You: Master the Elements of Style, Spirituality, and True Beauty* (New York: Simon and Schuster, 2010).

- The most important goal in choosing your outfit is that you feel you've nailed it. You are not allowed to feel unsure, insecure, uneasy, or uncomfortable in this outfit. This outfit screams you, and when you put it on, you are more confident, your posture improves, and your smile beams. This is the outfit that you move comfortably in and yet you feel elevated. If you have fabulous legs, highlight those; if you have a gorgeous décolletage, highlight that; and if you can choose an outfit that accentuates your waist, that is ideal. Sheer, silky material is sexy, and so is a structured waistline. Outfits are so individual because we have different sizes and shapes and moods and preferences. Take your time. Enjoy the process. Nail it. Keep note of the fact that in studies, brighter colors such as red, hot pink, and melon were perceived by men as sexier. Most importantly, this outfit—jumper, tracksuit, or minidress—must make you feel like your best you: confident, comfortable, and elevated.

"When in doubt, wear red." **Bill Blass**[75]

- *Sexy Shoes* – Now that you have your attire picked out, it's time to choose the right shoes to go with it. If you are going for that sexy look, you will want to consider pumps that show off your legs. Heels elongate the legs and make the ankles look leaner while causing the calves to appear more toned. Slender, toned, and well-defined legs are naturally attractive, and the shoes you choose can enhance this look.

75 Rosemarie Jarski, *Words from the Wise* (Skyhorse Publishing Inc., 2007).

"A woman can sexy, charming, witty, or shy with her shoes."
Christian Louboutin[76]

- To achieve a smooth, even look, celebrities use leg makeup—yes, body makeup—or very sheer nylons on the red carpet. Charlotte Tilbury® Supermodel Body Highlighter (charlottetilbury.com), MAC® Studio Face and Body (MAC.com), or Westmore Beauty® Body Coverage (westmorebeauty.com), in order of light to heavy coverage, are options celebrities use to walk the red carpet. Body makeup camouflages imperfections such as birthmarks, scars, or leg veins, and imparts a tan if you choose. Donna Karan® The Nudes Toeless sheer nylons are lovely for peep-toe pumps… and are so sheer that they give the legs an airbrushed look. For wrinkled knees or cellulite on the front of the thighs, celebrity stylists sometimes opt to use lift tapes. Skinnies® Instant Thigh Lifts (instantlifts.com) is a product that helps celebrities look their best under the scrutiny of harsh lighting. You can use the same tricks that they do to look your best. Harmonize your footwear with the dress you have chosen. You must be able to balance and walk with some confidence and swagger if you are to exude sexiness. One shoe trick I have learned for walking with poise is to insert leather Pedag® foot halters (Amazon.com) in the forefoot area. This not only cushions the bony area but allows a grip so that the foot does not slide forward in the

76 Sarah Kamali, "Christian Louboutin On Why Women Are 'Happy to Wear Painful Shoes.'" Huffington Post, 2011, retrieved from https://www.huffingtonpost.co.uk/2011/10/19/christian-louboutin-on-why-women-are-happy-to-wear-painful-shoes_n_7403680.html.

pump, causing awkwardness and blisters. This trick allows you to walk comfortably in shoes you may not have otherwise been able to wear. So: armed with all of this behind-the-scenes information, you are ready for some sexy shoes. Pumps are sexy, but of course knee boots, boots, ankle boots, and shoes of all sizes and colors can be sexy. The key is to be able to walk comfortably and *feel* sexy in your shoes.

"I really love over-the-knee boots. I think they're super sexy and they're fun. And they're also very strong and empowering." **Miranda Kerr**[77]

- *Accessories* – Don't forget to accessorize. Your choice in jewelry, purse, and other clothing accents can offer an opportunity to highlight your beauty and allure. Self-adornment is a sign of confidence in beauty, drawing attention to sensual sites, such as the neck, wrists, fingers. Cleopatra comes to mind as an iconic example. Choose a jewelry theme for the evening that harmonizes with your look. If your dress is bold, you may consider subtler pieces and vice versa if your dress is simple. In general, if the choice is silver versus gold, the main advice is to stay consistent. Also, accessorize in blocks of color (perhaps two or three that complement one another) instead of an array of different hues and tones. Last, try to have one "statement" piece of jewelry that makes an impression. This piece could have

77 Sarah Fogel, "The power of over the knee boots," HerCampus.com, 2015, retrieved from https://www.hercampus.com/school/trinity/power-over-knee-boots.

sentimental value or a symbol with deeper meaning to serve as a conversation starter. Though it makes a big statement, it need not be large. If you are married, consider wearing a piece from your first days of dating—to remind you both of the power of initial sexual excitement you enjoyed at that time.

- Outside of this, feel free to experiment with what makes you feel the most playful, fun, and flirtatious. Sexy jewels are often fine and sparkly. They lead the eye to places you would like your admirers to look—the plunging neckline or even a pretty piece worn to draw attention to your beautiful back. Sexy, shimmery anklets draw the eyes to the ankles and feet, possibly to the sexy footwear you have just chosen. Jewelry should enhance, not weigh down. Indeed, clutters of large jewelry pieces piled on top of one another might almost seem like a block, or an obstacle course instead of a lure. When your accessories are right, they add to how sexy you feel, and therefore look. Let your adornments boost your confidence to the next level. Check out *InStyle* magazine for suggestions. Sydney Evan (sydneyevan.com), Danielle Guizio (danielleguiziony.com), A. Marie Jewelry (amariejewelry.com), and Luv AJ (luvaj.com) are popular with celebrities at the moment.
- *Sexy Lingerie* – Being sexy does not necessarily include the intention to actually have sex. In fact, the most pleasurable part of sex is the anticipation of it and imagined scenarios about it. As the saying goes, "The largest sex organ is the brain." In other words, the *potential* sexual encounter is what captivates

us. Dressing in sexy underwear that is coordinated and fits nicely even if nobody but you know it, is part of feeling like a sexual powerhouse. It makes the possibility of sex more real, in a sense, and thus increases your sexual appeal. In other words, if you are flirting and strutting around in your fabulous outfit but you would never even dream of letting anyone see your (favorite comfy) tattered bra, you are being held back. Choose your lingerie and underwear with the idea that if layers were peeled back, you are truly sexy down to the skin and beyond. Imagine that your undergarments may be seen, and let your anticipatory imagination embolden you. Victoria's Secret is a great place to start by getting fitted for the correct bra size and then choosing from a panacea of colors and styles. It is best to try the undergarments on with the outfit you plan to wear in order to minimize creasing and BPLs (bad panty lines). For the next level, check out one of several shops that sell bolder lingerie. Agent Provocateur (agentprovacateur.com) in Beverly Hills is a local favorite for another level of sultry with added class.

- *Fragrances and Perfumes* – Are you shopping for fragrances and perfumes for your special evening ahead? Consider this…studies show that when it comes to aphrodisiacal properties, perfumes and colognes simply can't compete with easily accessible natural scents such as vanilla, cinnamon, licorice, and banana bread. Of course, the scent you choose to wear should be beautiful and make you feel beautiful, but if you can add in a moisturizer with one of the above-mentioned scents, you will be more alluring and approachable. I guess it's true what they say…the way to a man's heart is through his stomach. No wonder Bath & Body Works (bathandbodyworks.com) and Lush (lush.com) stores that specialize in delicious, sweet-scented soaps and creams are so popular. Whatever fragrances you select should not be overpowering or so bold as to distract attention from your overall impression. Remember that when compared to everything we have discussed, your natural scent has the greatest sex appeal.

Seven Days to Sexy – Day 4: Nails, Skin, and Smile

So, you're midway through your seven days to sexy. By now, you have invested a significant amount of time and energy into looking your best, and you are likely seeing the fruits of your labor. But there is more to be done. For Day 4, you will focus on your nails, smile, and skin, as these are important areas to highlight your beauty even further. Taking the time to have manicured nails…glowing, radiant skin…and a spectacular, dazzling smile is a simple way to heighten your attractiveness and beauty.

- *Manicures and Pedicures* – Well-groomed nails are a sign of health and youthfulness, and when it comes to sexy, making time for a mani-pedi is important. Some believe that bright red pointed nails are most sexy. Men were asked this question, and they consistently preferred natural colored, healthy-looking nails. In fact, in the majority of beauty photo shoots and fashion shows, the models wear natural pink or off-white colors with mid-length to short nails. Neutral-tone nail colors give the fingers an elongated look, and match any outfit. Remember that natural-looking manicured nails look healthy, and healthy is sexy. Because you already have a good idea of what you will be wearing, you may want to choose a color and style for your toes that further augments your look, particularly if you plan on wearing peep toe pumps. Again, self-care shows confidence, and confidence is sexy.

- *Teeth Whitening* – Beautifully white teeth and a dazzling smile are signs of good health, and likewise, they are universally attractive. With this in mind, ongoing dental care is required, but you can try a short-term technique to augment your pearly whites prior to a special occasion. Certainly, one good option involves visiting your dentist for a teeth-whitening appointment, but other options also exist. I have personally used Dr. George's Dental White system (www.drgeorges.com), which is a whitening gel that is effective and shows improvement in just a few treatments. It comes with simple trays that you mold to your teeth after warming. These and other options, such as Crest® Whitestrips from your local drugstore, allow you to quickly enhance the whiteness of your smile, so you can choose which one best meets your needs and schedule. Having a bright megawatt smile enhances your appeal and spreads joy.
- *Body Oils and Lotions* – Smooth, unblemished, soft skin reflects health and youthfulness as well as beauty. Therefore, being committed to skin care is an essential part of being and feeling attractive. Because the sun's rays can cause significant

damage to your skin's cells and structure, regular use of sunscreen is important. At the same time, moisturizing shaving gels, moisturizers, and body oils should be part of your daily routine. One lovely thing to do for skin hydration not long before your magical date is a sugar scrub. This moisturizes the skin, exfoliates, and leaves your skin smelling divine. My recent favorite is the Brazilian Cupuaçu Scrub in Oil by The Body Shop® (thebodyshop.com). This scrub could be an option on the day of your event, unless you have applied self-tanner or plan to wear body makeup. Likewise, not all skin types can handle an oil scrub. If you have acne-prone skin or bumpy skin (keratosis pilaris), you may consider Glytone® KP Kit instead. During your visit to the dermatologist or skin care professional, you may wish to have more specific advice tailored to your skin type and needs.

Seven Days to Sexy – Day 5: Hair and Waxing

> *"A good dose of healthy flirting makes me feel sexy, like I still have it. Shaving my legs makes me feel sexy too—it's such a small little thing."* **Katy Perry**[78]

The big day is getting close. Now it's time to focus on your hair and techniques that prepare you to be most attractive. Many options exist in this regard, and not all will apply to you. Choose from these hair

78 *Shape Magazine*, "What makes celebs feel sexy," n.d., retrieved from https://www.shape.com/celebrities/celebrity-photos/what-makes-celebs-feel-sexy.

care ideas that best fit your style and needs with the goal of having a healthy, shiny, sexy look in mind.

- *Hairstyle* – In general, flowing hair is the most appealing. Sexy hair comes in a variety of styles, and the one that makes you look and feel most beautiful is unique to you. Carefully consider the color, length, and cut in this regard. However, no matter the style you choose, your hair should look shiny, full of body, and have a healthy appearance. Dry, brittle hair is a hallmark of senescence and does not evoke a sexy vibe. Hairstyles with extensive hairspray to where the hair does not move are similarly less appealing. It is best to avoid drastic changes in your hair color or style right before your important date. This puts you at risk of frying your hair by overprocessing or not liking your hair color or cut. Bad hair can undermine your self-confidence. Don't be afraid to shake things up a little bit, though, to get a sense of freshness or novelty. Part of being your sexiest means expressing yourself in a variety of ways, and hairstyles offer that opportunity. Make your highlights a bit lighter or your brunette a little deeper…just enough to push the envelope of your look…to make a statement. On trend right now is the middle or side-of-middle part with beachy or smooth large waves. You can get this look with a large curling iron; and extensions never hurt, but we'll discuss that a bit later on. For best results, plan to get a blowout and style from your hairdresser on the day of the event.

- *Hair Treatments* – Enhancing and maintaining healthy, beautiful hair requires attention and some TLC. As a result, consider any of a number of hair treatments to help strengthen, protect, moisturize, and repair your hair. For example, several oils (such as argan oil and sunflower seed or macadamia oil products) can help produce smooth and silky hair. Other products help strengthen your hair's natural keratin structures to repair and prevent split ends and breakage, and polymer bond products can be applied to smooth out the cuticle of the hair and make it shine. Among local celebrities, the most popular items are weekly deep conditioning products such as Olaplex® (olaplex.com) that provide chemical buffers to your hair, and hair salon treatments such as Kérastase® (kerastase-usa.com) that systematically bathe, treat, and texturize your hair. Ask your hairdresser to help you choose salon-based and home-based regimens that are best for you.
- *Hair Extensions* – Damaged, thin, or short hair? No worries. Hair extensions or hair weaves can be used to create that sexy look that will drive men crazy. Several options exist, ranging from hair extensions that are taped in, clipped in, weaved, or fused with your normal hair. The safest for your hair are the clip-in temporary extensions that you can match to your hair color and use for events. Wigs Today, a store in Los Angeles, offers hundreds of hair extensions of varying color, texture, and length. You may try placing them at home with some practice, but professionals often place extensions more securely and

can style the pieces along with the rest of your hair for a more alluring and provocative look. You might be surprised how many women use hair extensions to augment their sex appeal. Most of female celebrities on the red carpet have extension pieces or a fall (single large extension across the back of the head) in place. Lighter pieces can be added to give a highlighted effect without damaging the hair with bleach. Most often extensions are placed not because the hair is damaged or thin, but instead to give that extra boost of volume and shine...a full bombshell effect. Christie Brinkley swears by hair extensions as being youth-enhancing, and she even has her own product line, Hair2Wear (hairuwear.com).

- *Waxing* – Removing body hair to create that smooth, sexy look can be part of your routine and is part of many women's practice on a regular basis. Waxing, to remove hair via hot or cold wax, has the advantage over shaving mainly in the length of time that unwanted hair remains absent. Most waxing procedures are effective for several weeks, and hair regrowth is often softer and less stubbly when compared to shaving. If you are prone to ingrown hairs or bumps, try Tend Skin® toner (Amazon.com) applied with a cotton ball to skin just after waxing. Another hair removal option is Nair® depilatory cream (naircare.com). Depilatory creams chemically melt hairs off, leaving the skin hairless but without razor burn. Of course, laser hair removal is often the best long-term hair removal option, but in the interest of time, waxing will have to do. If you plan to apply self-tanner before the big date, remember that waxing should come first.

Seven Days to Sexy – Day 6: Face, Body, and Cosmetics

Today is the perfect day to have a dry run to perfect your final look so that you are absolutely ready for the big day. This includes experimenting with cosmetic products as well as making time for makeovers, facials, and body care that make it easier on the following day to look your best.

- *Makeup* – Perhaps you already have your favorites, or it might be time to visit your beauty counter for additional advice and guidance on how to freshen up your look. Make an appointment at the MAC counter or simply pop in and see whether one of their makeup artists can show you new eye shadow and concealer tricks. Sephora offers similar services. It is not necessary to get out of your comfort zone too far...just enough to trigger a bit of excitement yet not enough to make you feel uncomfortable. My favorite base is Chanel® Vitalumière Aqua under Chanel Double Perfection compact matte powder. The most important thing about foundation is that it matches your skin tone perfectly. The latest trend is to add a shimmer with cheekbone highlighter from Jouer®, Laura Mercier® Shimmer Bloc or Charlotte Tilbury Bar of Gold (charlottetilbury.com). Also on trend right now is the thicker, darker dramatic brow. A definer such as Diorshow® Brow Styler works wonders, or some use John Frieda® Root Blur (johnfrieda.com) for stray grays on their head while applying some to their brows with a smaller brush. Dramatic thick lashes are always "in." Besides extensions or application of lashes, as we discussed before, my current favorite mascara is Miss Manga Mascara by L'Oreal® Paris because it thickens the lashes for a more dramatic look.

- There are thousands of types of makeup, therefore a trial and error approach is the best way to figure out which makeup matches your skin tone, doesn't cake or flake, and most importantly, does not cause a rash or breakouts. To this end, use moderation in experimenting with different looks right before your event if you have allergy-prone or acne-prone skin. Everything you choose should make you look and feel confident that you are putting your best face forward while enhancing and not masking your natural beauty. Remember that sultry red and pink tones draw longer attention to your lips—but sheer nude lips can be sexy as well.
- *Makeup Artist* – If time and budget allow, a makeup artist can transform your look for the evening. A practice run to make sure you like the style of the artist is a must. My favorite celebrity makeup artist is Troy Jensen (troyjensen.com). Depending on your location, you can use an online search or The Glam App (www.glamapp.com) to find a local makeup artist to help you get the perfect look.
- *Tanning and Bronzers* – Having a sun-kissed, glowing tan is associated with a healthy, sexy look. Its ability to mask skin imperfections, cellulite, and other blemishes makes it appealing,

but getting such a tan from the sun or from a tanning bed predisposes you to premature aging, sunspots, wrinkles, and skin cancer. The answer? Sunless tanners and skin bronzers. Many sunless tanners are now on the market ranging from sprays, to creams, to mousses, to gels. A popular brand celebs use at home is St. Tropez® Gradual Tan In Shower (Sephora.com). Jergens® Natural Glow is also popular as a tanning moisturizer that adds color gradually. Celebrities often go to spas that offer sunless tan airbrushing, and their favorite at-home product is Vita Liberata® Body Blur Instant HD that is routinely applied with their tanning mitt (Niemanmarcus.com).

- A few things to note, however...a self-tanner has a distinctive smell while it is processing, as the pigments are attaching themselves to your skin's keratin proteins. It is best not to apply self-tanner just before your event but instead on the days before. If applying a self-tanner, it is best to have exfoliated, clean, un-moisturized skin first. If there is a blunder or a streak, baking soda in water can remove it.
- Besides a self-tanner, body makeup is quite popular for photo shoots and on the red carpet. A favorite body makeup among celebrities is Westmore Beauty Body Coverage Perfector, which evens and balances skin color (westmorebeauty.com). MAC Studio Face and Body for legs and arms is also a popular option for achieving a perfectly smooth look...and Charlotte Tilbury Supermodel Body Slimmer Shimmer Shape can be applied over it. If your legs look great and you are looking to airbrush

your neck and décolletage, Dior® Air Flash is a wonderful option (Sephora.com).

- *Facial Treatments* – Unlike chemical peels, routine facials provided by estheticians provide a quick and effective means to enhance your appearance and eliminate unwanted blemishes in the skin. Through a multistep process that involves cleansers, steam, and masks, your face will be rejuvenated and appear healthier and more vibrant. Facials are ideal ways to achieve a more beautiful look quickly, and to appreciate the most advantage, you will choose to get one once a month or so. In our office, we offer deep pore cleansing facials that get in deep and clean out the pores and bumps from under the skin. These facials are workhorse facials that result in a bit of down time for a nice longer-term result. On the other hand, there are event facials that hydrate and soothe the skin while giving it a nice, taut appearance and a canvas ready for makeup. If your special day is close, I recommend an event facial rather than a deep cleansing facial, which is what our clients do right before appearances.

Her skin was alabaster white, smooth, milky—only a shade pinker than the sheet that she lay on. There was a white towel roll under her neck and white anti-puff patches under her eyes. Punctuating the whiteness of the scene was an unruly black pile of hair. On her mons pubis. I caught myself feeling a bit shocked. Although I have seen countless nude bodies,

I just wasn't expecting to walk in on one. She looked serene with her eyes closed and her body completely surrendered. She had turned her body over to her art—or at least—her beauty team's art. She lay motionless with her eyes closed, her notes dangling from her fingertips over the edge of the aesthetician table. Any anxiety that she seemed to have released was transferred to her assistant, assistant's assistant, facialist, makeup artist, hairdresser, and airbrush tan artist. In the meantime, my job was to inject a large pimple on her chin so that it would flatten out in time for her walk on the red carpet. I wondered whether I should address her directly. I mean, ironing her hair is one thing, but putting a shot in her chin is something else.

- *Nightmare pimple* – Often as you prepare for a big day or appearance, the stress gets to you, and suddenly a big, cystic pimple appears. The most common procedure we perform at our office for famous personalities is Kenalog® injections into pimples. When they get to be the size of Mount Vesuvius, they are impossible to conceal, so we shrink them with cortisone. The dose of cortisone is miniscule, but when injected right into the center of the pimple, it takes the swelling and tenderness down within twenty-four hours. We also offer Miracle Cream®, a topical anti-inflammatory that helps calm an inflamed pimple. When keeping your skin clean and cared for just isn't enough, you may have to touch base with your dermatologist for a pimple injection.

The ultimate goal in all these beauty-enhancing activities is to maximize self-confidence:

Many celebrities look beautiful but very human in real life. A few are absolute perfection regardless of hair, makeup, clothing. One such young woman who had won an international beauty pageant came to see me for a dimple in her thigh—a barely perceptible dimple. But this woman is under scrutiny every day, not only when she is seen at appearances, but when she is photographed for tabloids. Actually, that's not it: she was self-conscious about it. It was making her reluctant to do bikini modeling. I filled the dimple with hyaluronic filler, and later, for a more permanent fix we did CoolSculpting flat panel on her thigh—only half the normal duration of treatment since she was so thin. The dimple is gone and she is on the cover of a world-famous magazine wearing one. I see her now in the tabloids and on the runway—with her dimple-free thighs.

Seven Days to Sexy – Day 7: Confidence Boosting and Pregaming

> *"Happiness and confidence are the prettiest things you can wear"*—**Taylor Swift**[79]

On Days 1 through 6, you identified all those activities, procedures, and appointments you wanted to accomplish to make yourself as gorgeous as possible. You also purchased those items that would highlight your positives and minimize any features you felt were less desirable. And you hopefully had the opportunity to have a bit of a dry run, experimenting with new products along the way. By the time the big day comes, you have laid all the groundwork...you are prepared to be your absolute sexiest.

In terms of Day 7, one final thing remains...attitude. Attitude involves honing in that sense of confidence and that sexy persona that pulls everything together. Here are some key strategies and techniques you may want to consider as you approach those last few hours before you pull out all the stops.

> *"I had to grow to love my body. I did not have a good self-image at first. Finally, it occurred to me, I'm either going to love me or hate me. And I chose to love myself. Then everything kind of sprung from there. Things that I*

79 TaylorSwiftPlanet.com, "Taylor Swift quotes," n.d., retrieved from http://www.taylorswift-planet.com/taylor-swift-quotes.html.

thought weren't attractive became sexy. Confidence makes you sexy." **Queen Latifah**[80]

- *Sleep Well* – Getting adequate sleep the night before a special occasion helps you think clearly and have a bright, alert look while minimizing dark circles under the eyes. Limit salt intake before bed, and you may even want to take your vitamins just before bedtime, to reduce puffiness. If you have trouble sleeping, consider taking a small dose of melatonin.
- *Hydrate* – Drink plenty of water and stay hydrated throughout the day. Hydration helps all your tissues look their healthiest and most radiant.
- *Plan the Little Things* – From transportation to the time needed to get ready for the event, plan your schedule and any of the other things you may need so you can eliminate any unnecessary stresses and worries. Know more about the place you are going and the people who will be at the event you are attending. A few little tidbits of information can help you make conversation, and to feel and look composed. Make sure that your car and your personal space is neat, clean, and smells divine...just in case.
- *Positive Affirmations* – Repeat those mantras that help you know how beautiful and attractive you are both inside and out.
- *Get Your Sexy On!* – Don't forget about those pregame activities that help boost your confidence and self-esteem while getting you in the mood for a potential encounter. Remember a few

80 Uncustomary.com, "30 quotes about self-love," 2015, retrieved from http://uncustomary.org/30-quotes-about-self-love/.

of the sexy moves we discussed earlier—so that you can use them later this evening. Is there a particular song that makes you feel sexy? Perhaps a glass of wine (just one—if you are not driving) would make you feel a bit more brazen?

As you leave to meet that special someone, attend an event, or simply go out to socialize, cast aside your insecurities. Be bold. Despite having only seven days to prepare, you have done all the preparations to enhance your sex appeal and appearance. From your head down to your toes you feel awesome…you exude self-confidence…and you look absolutely stunning. Now, all you have to do is sit back and enjoy the ride. By employing the *Seven Days to Sexy* approach, your encounter begins with all the potential in the world…anything could happen. So, let the excitement consume you and let your mind be filled with fantasies. You *ARE* your sexiest self, and others cannot help but notice.

Chapter 5
Seven Weeks to Sexy

Have you ever found yourself in a situation in high school or college where you had to cram for a test for which you were poorly prepared? Maybe you had too heavy of a course load that semester, or you simply indulged in some other more exciting things to do. After all, life is short. But at some point, you had to face the music...you needed to pass the final exam to pass the course. Otherwise, you might find yourself back the next semester taking the same course all over again. So, you hunkered down, made sure you had a steady supply of caffeine, and tried to learn everything you needed to know about the subject in the matter of a few days.

Seven Days to Sexy is kind of like cramming for that exam. In a short amount of time, you achieve what needs to be done as quickly as possible. And, like cramming for the test, it works. But at the same time, if you had prepared throughout the semester for the final exam, you would have achieved even better results and higher course scores all along the way. Well, guess what? The same applies to your efforts in looking your best. Though much can be accomplished in seven days, even more can be achieved over seven weeks. And when you invest a longer period of time in your health, beauty, and level of attractiveness, you get to enjoy being sexy all along the way... whenever you decide to turn it on.

In this chapter, we will focus on the activities and exercises you may consider for a more long-term approach to being as beautiful and appealing as you can be. Some of the activities involve procedures that take longer to realize effects or that require longer healing periods. Others include lifestyle changes that require time to become a routine part of your life to provide noticeable results. In pursuing these activities, you take a more long-term and holistic approach in being your best. Whether you were motivated by the impressive results provided in your "seven days to sexy" routine, have a longer amount of time before an important event, or simply want to pull out all the stops, Seven Weeks to Sexy offers a more permanent and enduring strategy for you to be your absolute sexiest.

Seven Weeks to Sexy – Step 1: Appointments and Procedures

The weekly approach to being your most attractive and beautiful allows you additional time to reap the maximum benefits from whatever regimen you choose to pursue. However, instead of listing activities that should be performed each day or week, Seven Weeks to Sexy provides seven steps to perform during this time. To receive the most from your efforts, consider all the steps for the entire period rather than on a week-to-week basis. Having said this, however, the first week does require setting up appointments, memberships, and other activities that you are considering over the course of the next several weeks so that you will have adequate time to realize the benefits or potentially heal from any procedure. The following are some specific ***consults and appointments*** that you may want to arrange during your first week so you can begin your pursuit of sexy as soon as possible.

- *Dermatology, Aesthetician, and Plastic Surgery Consultations* – These specialists and experts offer a range of expertise regarding lifestyle changes as well as various procedures and activities that can enhance your beauty and sexiness. Likewise, these professionals can provide excellent guidance regarding overall skin care. Some of the activities to be described in this chapter will require their assistance, but at the same time, arranging a consult with these specialists can help you better understand the options available to you while educating you about their advantages and disadvantages in the process.
- *Gym, Trainer, and Fitness Club Appointments and Memberships* – As you move from cramming for the test to investing in a more long-term approach to sexy, physical exercise and fitness becomes increasingly important. This not only pertains to physical appearance but also mental attitude and levels of confidence. There is a catch, though. In order to reap these benefits, you have to attend. Make appointments to check out local gyms, Pilates courses, yoga studios, and personal trainers. Discuss your goals and preferences and see which options are best for you. Once exercise becomes a routine part of your lifestyle (if it isn't already), you will clearly see the impact this has on health, beauty, and overall sex appeal.

- *Dietician and Nutrition Consultations* – Certainly, not everyone needs to consider nutrition appointments and consultations, but they can be quite helpful when special dietary needs exist, targeted goals are important, and when a long-term diet plan is a must. At the same time, one-time consults can be extremely educational and put you on the right track to being healthy. Specific guidance regarding diet and nutrition will be provided in this chapter also, but these appointments may be worth considering in some instances.

In addition to appointment scheduling, you might also consider any of several beauty-enhancing procedures during Week 1. Procedures that take a little longer to heal or to provide their optimal results should be arranged sooner rather than later. In doing so, you will allow enough time to pass so that you can enjoy their benefits fully and look absolutely amazing in the process.

- *CoolSculpting®* – CoolSculpting is an FDA-approved, nonsurgical procedure that allows you to reshape your contours while essentially freezing your fat away in those hard-to-get-rid-of areas. You know the ones…those little pockets of fat in your thighs, hips, and other areas that persist no matter how much you diet and exercise. CoolSculpting allows you to get rid of bulges without damaging the skin or requiring any type of surgery. How awesome is that! Unlike other activities that reduce the size of existing fat cells, CoolSculpting actually reduces the number of fat cells permanently by freezing them underneath the skin.

As fat cells are frozen, they die and are eventually removed from the body permanently. For this reason, the optimal effect is usually seen over two to three months, and depending on the areas you wish to target, more than one day of treatment may be required. Regardless, CoolSculpting is a great way to get that sexy shape you want in a safe and effective way. With over five million CoolSculpting procedures performed worldwide, this beauty procedure has proven itself repeatedly. This is a great way to optimize that waist-to-hip ratio and boost confidence.

- *Laser Hair Removal* – Unwanted hair can be a problem when your goal is to be sexy. Keeping that smooth, sleek look is hard enough when considering your legs and under the arms, but when unibrows, shaded upper lips, and facial hair are also an issue, personal hygiene is even more of a pain. Laser hair removal is an excellent option when it comes to these issues. By destroying hair follicles with a highly concentrated laser, most women can achieve permanent hair loss in these areas. Because lasers are attracted to darker pigments, women with darker, coarser hair and fairer skin are the best candidates, but all women may have some benefit from this treatment. Laser hair removal has minimal discomfort (similar to being popped with a rubber band), and it only takes minutes to perform. And while some immediate results are apparent, maximum effect usually takes one to three weeks before unwanted hair falls out, leaving smooth, silky, and hairless skin. A series of six to eight treatments are often required.

- *Photofacials* – Photofacials, which are also called photo-rejuvenation, use light therapy to enhance the skin and the appearance of your face. Wrinkles, age spots, sun spots, and other blemishes can be reduced or eliminated through these therapies. In essence, two types of photofacial options exist. The first involves Intense Pulsed Light, or IPL, which was discussed in the section on Seven Days to Sexy, but it should also be included in your Seven Weeks to Sexy plan since more than one session is often helpful. The other type of photofacials involve LED light. LED (light emitting diode) is less intense than IPL, but it also stimulates collagen production to reduce wrinkles, smooth the skin, and provide a more youthful appearance to the face. LED photofacials usually consist of twelve weekly to bimonthly sessions.
- *Fraxel® Laser*– What do you think of when you heard the word "Fraxel?" It's kind of like combining the words "fragments" and "pixelated," which helps you better appreciate how this therapy works. Fraxel therapy provides tiny fragments of laser treatments to the skin resulting in microscopic areas of thermal injury. This may not sound too wonderful, but in doing so, it stimulates collagen production and creates smoother, tighter, and more radiant skin. Typically, the Fraxel laser works best for wrinkles, enlarged pores, and some pigmented skin spots, and it can require a series of four to six monthly treatments. While it is a bit more painful than IPL and LED light therapies and requires a few days for recovery, it is a more effective

way to truly change and enhance the beauty of your skin. It is recommended as a series (four to six treatments) one month apart. Speaking with your dermatologist can help you decide whether Fraxel is an ideal treatment for your skin type and beauty goals.

- *Thermage®* – This treatment is an excellent choice for lifting the brow, eyelids, and jawline, as well as for eliminating facial wrinkles. Thermage is an FDA-approved radiofrequency therapy, which means it uses radiofrequency energy to stimulate the dermal layer of the skin. In doing so, it causes tightening of existing collagen fibers and stimulates new collagen production. The end result? Tighter, smoother skin. The best thing about Thermage is that it is noninvasive, causes minimal discomfort, takes only a couple of hours, and usually lasts for a couple of years. Likewise, one treatment is often effective, and any redness that develops in response to the treatment typically goes away in a few minutes. Though the full effect often takes up to six months to see, Thermage is an excellent consideration for many women wanting to have a more glowing and youthful look to their skin and face.
- *VelaShape® Therapy* – No one likes cellulite. That dimpled, orange peel look is universally unattractive, yet it is extremely common among women in certain trouble areas. You know the ones…the thighs, hips, and buttocks. VelaShape offers a noninvasive way to reduce cellulite while also helping recontour those curves. By applying a combination of infrared light,

radiofrequency waves, and a suctioning vacuum, VelaShape cuts cellulite by typically more than half while slimming the circumference of specific body areas. While the vacuum component brings fat cells closer to the skin, the infrared light and radiofrequency waves provide a deep heat to fatty tissue resulting in collagen and elastin stimulation. This results in smoother and more youthful looking skin while letting you restore those feminine contours that make you look your sexiest. Each VelaShape session lasts about half an hour and feels like a warm deep tissue massage, and most women see results after three to six sessions. VelaShape is used in tissues under the chin and in the arms, legs, buttocks, and abdomen, and is an affordable beauty procedure with essentially no down time. Though the results are not permanent, they can be preserved with maintenance treatments. Other options for permanent cellulite improvement are the CoolSculpting flat panel, and Cellfina®, a surgical option that untethers skin connections to the dimples.

Seven Weeks to Sexy – Step 2: Skin and Facial Care

Did you know your skin is the largest organ in the body? While our skin is our barrier to the world, it is also so much more. The way our skin and face appear tells others a great deal about our health and well-being. And of course, it says a lot about beauty. The saying, "Beauty is more than skin deep" is quite relevant here, because the condition of your skin reflects what is going on internally. Given more time than a few days, you can take several steps to enhance the glow and attractiveness of your skin by investing in the right care products and a necessary amount of time. Once you have employed such efforts for several weeks, you will be amazed at the results. But before you can take the right approach to having beautiful skin, you need to know a little about your own.

Skin can be classified into six different types...normal, dry, oily, combination, sensitive, and aging. Knowing which skin type you have makes a significant difference in what products you need, how they are used, and the overall regimen you pursue in enhancing your skin's appearance and glow. So which type do you have? The following provides a description of the six skin types and the optimal beauty regimen to consider when striving to have skin that is smooth, silky, radiant, and therefore sexy.[81] These skin regimens can change with time. New products and discoveries arise daily. The advice below is what I recommend today, at the time of writing these recommendations. Check in at www.bellaskininstitute.com or follow @annaguanchemd and @bellaskininstitute on Instagram for updated skin care advice.

Normal skin type – People with this skin type are the envy of everyone. As Goldilocks might say, "Not too dry, not too oily, not too sensitive...just right." For normal skin types, the following regimen and products are encouraged:

- Morning care: It is best to use a mild cleanser such as Cetaphil® gentle cleanser or our favorite SkinCeuticals® foaming cleanser

81 Faith Xue, "The exact regimen you should be following for every skin type," Birdie.com website, 2017, retrieved from http://www.byrdie.com/daily-skincare-routine/slide6.

that provides a mild lather. Also, a light skin moisturizer with SPF protection should be included that contains hyaluronic acid, dimethicone, and/or panthenol to enhance hydration. A recommended brand of SPF is Alastin® Hydratint Pro Mineral Broad-Spectrum Sunscreen.

- Evening care: The same cleanser can be used as described above with a non-SPF moisturizer as well as an antioxidant serum. An effective serum that I recommend is iS Clinical® Super Serum that combines 15 percent vitamin C and copper tripeptide growth factors as well as botanical antioxidants. Antioxidants stave off aging by quenching oxygen free radicals created by UV exposure. A light moisturizer with actives as well is Alastin restorative skin complex. Another moisturizer option for normal skin is Avene® Hydrance Light.
- Weekly care: The use of a glycolic acid treatment weekly helps keep normal skin problem free, as these tiny molecules are able to travel deep into the skin, providing moisture and microexfoliation to prevent congested pores. A favorite glycolic acid product is Jan Marini® Bioglycolic Face Cream.

Dry skin type – If you have dry skin, the moisture barrier that should ideally be in place is often damaged in some way, causing tiny, invisible cracks in the skin that enable moisture to escape from the skin. Often this skin type is predisposed to eczema and rashes. For dry skin types, the following regimen and products are encouraged:

- <u>Morning care:</u> Like normal skin, a mild cleanser such as Cetaphil Gentle Cleanser or SkinCeuticals Gentle Cleanser should be used daily. Select a cleansing lotion that does not foam and does not cause a great deal of lather, since foaming agents often reduce your natural skin oils. The use of a hydrating serum such as SkinCeuticals B5 Hydrating Gel followed by a moisturizing SPF, such as Alastin Hydratint Pro Mineral Broad-Spectrum Sunscreen or Elta MD® UV Daily Broad-Spectrum SPF 40, is ideal.
- <u>Evening care</u>: The same cleanser described above with a non-SPF moisturizer such as iS Clinical Youth Intensive Crème should be part of your evening regimen. In addition, hydrating eye balms such as Neocutis® Lumière Riche creams can help boost collagen around the eyes. For extreme dryness, our patients swear by Bio-Oil Purcellin Oil.

  Another option for extra hydration is a layer of Alastin Regenerating Skin Nectar under your moisturizer. Vitamin A derivatives, such as Retin-A and retinol, should be used very gradually and with caution in dry skin types, as they can exacerbate dryness in the short term.
- <u>Weekly care</u>: Dry skin results in a higher number of dead skin cells, and gentle exfoliation with iS Clinical Tri-Active Exfoliant once weekly can be useful. If your skin is sensitive, try a hydrating mask to soothe it.

Oily skin type – If you have oily skin, the larger oil glands and higher sebum content present were likely inherited. While you can't change your genetic makeup, you can employ several strategies for more beautiful skin. For oily skin types, the following regimen and products are encouraged:

- Morning care: Selection of a cleanser should involve the use of exfoliating agents such as glycolic acid, an active ingredient in SkinCeuticals LHA Cleanser. For acne-prone skin, a bit of trial and error may be necessary, or consider a consultation with a dermatologist. A toner with drying agents such as SkinCeuticals Biomedic Conditioning Solution offers another level of cleanliness to the skin. For oily skin types, the choice of an SPF is important, since it should not be thick or greasy. Elta MD UV Clear Broad-Spectrum SPF 46, tinted or clear, is a great option since it does not block the pores. Consider adding a coat of OC8® Professional Mattifying Gel over the SPF or over your makeup to reduce that oily shine.
- Evening care: For the evening, use the same cleansing gel and toner, but also include a light, oil-free moisturizer such as Avene Hydrance Light. For oily skin, consider adding a vitamin A derivative such as Retin-A Rx or retinol products before your moisturizer to reduce oil production. Alastin Renewal Retinol is also one option.
- Weekly care: Using a clay or activated charcoal mask once a week can further help manage excessively oily skin, but the key is not to leave these treatments on too long. These masks

can exfoliate and pull out comedones (blackheads) and thus improve the appearance of the skin. It is important to follow instructions carefully for at-home masks so that the skin does not become raw and irritated.

Combination skin type – What is combination skin type? Just what you might expect…some spots are a little dry…other spots are a little oily. Overall, skin and facial care is similar to the dry skin regimen:

- Morning care: Like normal skin, a mild cleanser such as Cetaphil Gentle Cleanser or SkinCeuticals Gentle Cleanser should be used daily. Select a cleansing lotion that does not foam and does not cause a great deal of lather, since foaming agents often reduce your natural skin oils. The use of a hydrating serum such as SkinCeuticals B5 Hydrating Gel followed by a moisturizing SPF, such as Alastin Hydratint Pro Mineral Broad-Spectrum Sunscreen or Elta MD UV Daily Broad-Spectrum SPF 40, is ideal.
- Evening care: The same cleanser described above with a non-SPF moisturizer, such as iS Clinical Youth Intensive Crème, should be part of your evening regimen. In addition, hydrating eye balms, such as Neocutis Lumière Riche cream, can help boost collagen around the eyes. For extreme dryness, our patients swear by Bio-Oil Purcellin Oil.

  Another option for extra hydration is a layer of Alastin Regenerating Skin Nectar under your moisturizer. Use vitamin

A derivatives, such as Retin-A and retinol, with caution only in the oily T-zone of the face.

- Weekly care: Dry skin results in a higher number of dead skin cells, and gentle exfoliation with iS Clinical Tri-Active Exfoliant once weekly could be useful. If your skin is sensitive, try a hydrating mask to soothe it. Usually the midface is still oily in combination skin, so use of charcoal or clay masks is recommended only in the oily areas. Again, OC8 Professional Mattifying gel can help reduce shine in oily areas.

Sensitive skin type – If you have sensitive skin, you appreciate that it is more prone to being irritated and inflamed. Many people who are labeled as having sensitive skin actually have rosacea or allergies. Therefore, the rule is to provide gentle care regimens in order to reduce irritation and redness:

- <u>Morning care:</u> For sensitive skin, use a mild cleanser such as Cetaphil Gentle Cleanser or La Roche Posay® Tolariane Hydrating Gentle Cleanser. For reducing redness and heat in the skin, I recommend Avene Antirougers Redness Relief Dermo-Cleansing Milk. This, followed by iS Clinical Pro Heal Serum, helps improve the skin barrier. Avene Antirougers Day SPF 25 is a great option for sunscreen. Alternatively, La Roche Posay Rosaliac CC cream offers SPF 30 protection as well as a camouflage tint.
- <u>Evening care</u>: The regimen here is simple...use the same cleansing lotion, serum, and Avene Antirougers as a nighttime

moisturizer. For skin that is chronically sensitive, red, peely, or bumpy, you may need to see a dermatologist to tailor a prescription-strength skin treatment regimen for you.

- Weekly care: Consider using an anti-inflammatory soothing face mask once a week for sensitive skin. Avene Antirouger Calm is a great option.

Aging skin type – Wrinkles, loose skin, and brown spots characterize aging skin, as many women know all too well. Thus, products that help combat these time-sensitive changes are recommended to enhance your youthful appearance. Of course, there are a panacea of antiaging skin creams to choose from. New products are arriving on the scene daily. Some are proven over time and with feedback from those who use them, so I will mention my favorites here with the understanding that new and better products are always on the horizon. Also, an examination by a skin specialist, who tailors a skin care regimen specific to your skin type, concerns and budget, is always best.

- Morning care: Mild cleansers are what I recommend in general, since some of the antiaging active ingredients that I advise for the evening may cause peeling in the first six weeks. SkinCeuticals Gentle Cleanser or Cetaphil Gentle Cleanser are great options. Apply an antioxidant serum, such as iS Clinical Super Serum Advance or iS Clinical Youth Serum, after the face is dry. An important step is to apply sunscreen to prevent further photodamage. For daily wear, Alastin Hydratint Pro Mineral

Broad-Spectrum Sunscreen or Elta MD UV Clear Broad-Spectrum SPF 46 are advisable.

- Evening care: The same mild cleanser can be used as highlighted above. After the face is dry, I recommend a vitamin A derivative called tretinoin. This is a prescription-strength cream that is the most powerful antiaging topical treatment known to date. I have used it myself every night for over twenty years. It can be combined with hydroquinone and/or kojic acid to brighten brown spots or melasma pigmentation. If you are unable to get a prescription for these items, then retinol, a precursor to tretinoin, will do. It is converted on the skin to tretinoin via an enzymatic process, creating a variable dosing on the skin. Because of the retinoid reaction, which causes redness and peeling in the first few weeks, it is important to use sunscreen in the morning and a great moisturizer just after application in the evening. iS Clinical Youth Intensive Crème or SkinCeuticals AGE Interrupter are both strongly hydrating moisturizers that help combat the dryness and peeling during this phase.
- Neck, Chest, and Hands: An important part of antiaging skin care is to address the neck, chest, and hands. Over time, great skin care on the face leaves the skin looking dramatically younger than the hands, neck, and chest. To avoid contrast between face and body, these often-exposed areas should get a coat of daily sunscreen (whichever you choose for your face) and a coat of Nectifirm® or Alastin Restorative Neck Complex for the front of the neck.

- Monthly care: The use of facial peels such as Jessner's and brightening microdermabrasion treatments such as Silkpeel Dermalinfusion® can further help rejuvenate your skin and facial appearance when performed on a regular basis. Depending on your underlying skin type (prior to developing an aging skin type), you may choose to try facials that enhance your skin's health, clarity, and beauty.

Seven Weeks to Sexy – Step 3: Hair Care

> "*When do I feel sexiest? When I get out of the shower and I feel fresh and my hair is clean. I feel very sexy then because I'm so clean and pure and beautiful.*" **Fergie**[82]

Wouldn't it be nice to have soft, shiny, bouncy hair all the time? Depending on the type of hair you have, this can be challenging. But there is good news. With a consistent regimen of hair care over several weeks, you *CAN* enjoy beautiful, sexy hair. The key is knowing what hair type you have, how often to wash and condition, and which additives and supplements to use. Believe it or not, having awesome hair is not as hard as you might think, and by following these Seven Weeks to Sexy hair care tips, you can improve the look and texture of your hair.

Before discussing a specific hair care regimen for you, knowing a little about shampoos and conditioners can go a long way in helping

82 *Shape Magazine*, "What makes celebs feel sexy," n.d., retrieved from https://www.shape.com/celebrities/celebrity-photos/what-makes-celebs-feel-sexy.

you decide which products might be best. After all, most hair shampoos and conditioners have an array of ingredients that you may or may not recognize. While knowing all the chemicals and compounds is not necessary, some basic understanding about the purpose of these common ingredients and their effect can be helpful. Likewise, the use of additional hair care products (like oils and hair nutrients) can offer greater progress in achieving that look you want long term.

Shampoos and Conditioners – Let's start with the basics. Everyone appreciates that shampoos cleanse the hair while conditioners help restore your hair's contour, shine and manageability. But within each of these products, a variety of chemicals are typically present. For example, shampoos are made of detergents that bind oil and dirt while allowing these substances to be easily washed away with water. But at the same time, detergents deplete your hair of its natural oils and can cause damage to the hair shaft, and this can result in frizzy hair as well as split ends. Conditioners thus attempt to replenish these oils while protecting the hair from damage and excessive drying. The first rule of thumb...always condition whenever you wash.

When washing your hair with shampoo, be sure to concentrate on your scalp rather than on the hair itself. Your scalp is not only where your hair follicles are but also where cleaning is needed the most. In contrast, concentrate conditioning on the tips of your hair where damage and split ends are more likely to occur. Since your natural hair oils will be replenished from the area of the hair follicles first, your hair farthest away from the scalp will be the part most vulnerable.

Following this basic approach during your routine hair care will help promote the healthiest hair possible.

In addition to these basic rules, it is also important to make sure your shampoo and conditioner are both pH balanced. If the pH is too high, then hair follicles swell, and the cuticle of your hair shaft opens, and this is never a good thing. Most shampoos use glycolic acid or citric acid to ensure the pH is low enough to allow your hair follicles to function normally. This can be even more important for hair that has been chemically treated. Also, if you live in an area that has hard water, the detergents in shampoos can react with the magnesium and calcium in the water to create an unwanted coating on your hair making it dull and opaque. Choosing a shampoo with a sequestering agent (like EDTA or sodium triphosphate) can avoid this problem.

Interestingly, most of the other ingredients in these products have little if any effect on cleansing or protecting your hair. Thickeners, preservatives, foaming agents, and other additives are included to enhance the visual appeal of the product or to prolong its shelf life. While preservatives are important to prevent germ contamination or product decomposition, the other ingredients are less so. Focus on the other key ingredients, and select products designed for your hair type, and you will be much more likely to get the results you want.[83]

Hair Care Additives – Many hair care additives are available for you to consider, whether they are directly applied to your hair or included as part of your diet and nutrition. Beginning with your diet, several

83 Paschal D'Souza and Sanjay K. Rathi, "Shampoo and conditioners: What a dermatologist should know?" *Indian Journal of Dermatology* 60, no. 3 (2015): 248.

supplements have been shown to support hair growth and health. For example, fish oil (rich in omega-3s and omega-6s) helps prevent hair loss while biotin, pantothenic acid, and glucosamine can stimulate hair growth. Zinc supplements help hair follicle function because zinc is a required substance for many hair follicle enzymes. Other vitamins like vitamin E and vitamin C also help repair damage to the hair follicle while protecting it from inflammation. These, along with vitamin D, should be included as part of your hair care regimen on a routine basis when striving to keep your hair healthy and beautiful.[84] Our favorite hair growth supplement is Viviscal® PRO, a high-dose biotin and marine extract supplement that has worked consistently for our patients. Another helpful supplement is JarroSil® bioavailable silicon drops that provide raw materials for the hair sheath. These promote healthy hair with good caliber and shine.

Other additives can be applied directly to the hair to help promote good health and beauty. For example, coconut oil, sunflower oil and mineral oil help replenish the loss of natural oils from the hair and thus reduce drying, split ends, and hair damage. Coconut oil specifically has also been shown to promote glossiness of the hair. Brazilian oils and butters also can provide similar benefits. And aloe vera applications in various forms supply your hair with many nutrients and protections to give it a healthy, shiny glow.[85] Based on your specific hair type,

84 Josh Axe, "Top 6 vitamins for hair growth," 2016, retrieved from https://draxe.com/vitamins-for-hair-growth/.

85 Maria Fernanda Reis Gavazzoni Dias, "Hair cosmetics: an overview," *International Journal of Trichology* 7, no. 1 (2015): 2.

you can determine which of these products are most important and include them in your daily routine.

Hair Types and Hair Care Guidelines – In the same way your specific skin type dictates the type of beauty regimen used, your hair type does as well. Depending on whether your hair is straight, wavy, loosely curled, or tightly curled, different hair care routines are encouraged to maximize the look and health of your hair.[86]

- Straight Hair: With straight hair, the natural oils have no trouble reaching the ends of the strands, and therefore, this hair type is often more tolerant to cleansing than other types. In general, washing your hair every other day is fine, and as always, apply conditioner with every wash. Comb regularly to help distribute your natural hair oils as much as possible, and deep condition (which requires leaving conditioner in place for twenty to thirty minutes) monthly. Olaplex® and Kérastase® deep conditioners are two products that have given our patients excellent results. Challenges for straight hair can involve a lack of volume and bounce, particularly in areas closest to the scalp. Blow-drying your hair while using a rounded brush and holding your head upside down are two effective techniques to overcome these problems.
- Wavy Hair: This hair type is not as challenging as curly hair, but it is more prone to dryness and damage when compared

86 Shilpi Tomar, "The perfect hair care routine for every hair type," Madison-Reed.com, 2017, retrieved from https://www.madison-reed.com/blog/the-perfect-hair-care-routine-for-every-hair-type.

to straight hair. Cleansing your hair two to three times a week is thus recommended instead of every other day, and deep conditioning should be performed twice a month. If needed, dry shampoo can be applied in between regular washings. Kevin Murphy® Doo Over is a wonderful dry shampoo that works by cutting oils while leaving the hair smelling lovely. If frizziness is a problem, leave-in conditioners, such as Kevin Murphy Leave-In Repair or Smooth Again, promote a healthy sheen.

- Curly Hair: With this hair type, it is more challenging for your hair's natural oils to reach the tips of the strands, and therefore, dryness, frizziness, and split ends are more common. Cleansing should be limited to once or twice a week, and deep conditioning should be performed weekly. Likewise, leave-in conditioners are beneficial on a more regular basis. And most importantly, be sure to apply a heat-protective hair spray such as Joico® K-Pak Protective Hairspray prior to blow-drying your hair.
- Tight Curly/Coily Hair: This hair type poses some of the toughest challenges. While body and bounce are rarely a problem, hair strands tend to be much more fragile and prone to dryness and damage. As a result, limit cleansing to once a week and use a gentle conditioner to avoid hair damage. Prior to cleansing, the use of a hot oil treatment may be helpful, and afterward, the application of heavy oils or coating butters such as Bumble and Bumble® Hairdresser's Invisible Dry Oil Finishing Spray can provide further protection. As a general rule, the less heat applied to this hair type, the better.

Seven Weeks to Sexy – Step 4: Body Shaping and Exercise

> *"I'm at my sexiest right after I leave the gym. I always feel so good; I also like being glammed up, though. Every girl has their insecurities, but I've become more comfortable with my body as I've grown older."* **Kim Kardashian**[87]

Are you ready to whip that body into shape? Within several weeks, you can see amazing results in your physique by incorporating a bit of exercise. And if your time is limited, other beauty strategies can also be used to enhance your shapely figure. The more time you invest in a healthy body, the better the results. Therefore, it only stands to reason that adopting a lifestyle that includes exercise and body toning will pay great dividends over time. But there is more to body shaping and exercise than just physical fitness and a sexy shape. The effects these activities have on our psyche is tremendous, and these effects are also cumulative over time.

With this in mind, activities that foster a gorgeous shape while boosting your confidence are some of the best ways to be your most alluring and attractive self. Activities like yoga and Pilates let you improve not only on your balance, posture, flexibility, and strength, but they also provide a mind-body connection important for pursuing holistic health and beauty. At the same time, cross-training with aerobic and cardio fitness activities helps you have higher levels of energy, better circulation, and a body that is toned and defined. Your

87 *Shape Magazine*, "What makes celebs feel sexy," n.d., retrieved from https://www.shape.com/celebrities/celebrity-photos/what-makes-celebs-feel-sexy.

skin, muscles, and shape will naturally be more attractive as a result while helping you achieve the weight and health you desire.

A word about corset training should also be mentioned. While some of the benefits of waist trainers and corsets can be seen within days of wearing them, more pronounced effects are often realized over a six- to eight-week period. While the circumference of your hips won't change (since the hip bones are more or less fixed), the shape of the lower ribs and abdominal tissues can respond, making your waist smaller and giving you more of that hourglass look. In a similar way that the body magically spreads out to make space for a baby, it can also be gradually pulled in by gentle retraining. The key is to not overtighten the corset. Wearing a corset should feel like someone is giving you a tight hug, but actual pain and discomfort should not be present. I do not recommend using the corset during exercise, but instead, I encourage use while relaxing in the evening or a few hours each night at bedtime. Standing for longer periods of time with a corset in place can increase venous pressure in the legs, leading to swelling or worse…leg veins.

The following is a summary of various body shaping and exercise activities to consider during your Seven Weeks to Sexy routine.

- <u>Yoga</u> – Yoga provides an excellent holistic exercise with a focus on strength, flexibility, balance, and mind-body connections. This activity should be routinely performed biweekly or more for progressive physical and mental benefits. What do Adam Levine, Jessica Biel, and Gisele Bündchen have in common? They all do yoga. Yoga is sexy! Yoga adds a mystique to your persona. Your posture and poise are excellent, your gratitude intact, and your yoga butt is on point. The calm and internal balance that yoga gives you adds to your confidence. Yoga is the science of happiness, and happiness is very attractive. A lithe, strong, flexible body is a sexy body.

"*Yoga makes me feel really sexy.*" **Alicia Silverstone**[88]

- Pilates – Pilates is an exercise program that also offers enhanced strength, balance, endurance, and flexibility. Pilates also requires an intense concentration of control of movements, breathing, and posture that further promote fitness and confidence, and it selectively targets core areas, allowing for better waist contouring. Madonna, Gwyneth Paltrow, and Uma Thurman are just a few of the celebrity beauties who do Pilates.
- Aerobic activities – Cardio and aerobic activities enhance your circulation, tissue oxygenation, and wellness while also promoting healthy weight management and a healthy heart. Select different activities and intensities based on your needs (fat burning versus endurance building). Activities range from jogging, to cycling, to swimming, to many others depending on your interests and preferences.
- Weight training – Well-defined muscles that are sleek and toned are naturally attractive. Weight training can thus offer some advantages here while also building strength and endurance.

88 Jennifer Kasle Furmaniak, "Fun, Fearless Female of the Year 2004: Alicia Silverstone," *Cosmopolitan*, 2004, retrieved from https://www.cosmopolitan.com/entertainment/celebs/news/a1598/alicia-silverstone/.

Ideal approaches in achieving that sexy look typically use low weights with high repetitions. And, of course, take precautions to avoid injuries caused by lifting too much weight too quickly. Weight (resistance) training increases bone mass and staves off osteoporosis.

- Corset Training – This body-shaping activity reduces waist circumference while molding the abdomen and lower ribs into an hourglass shaped figure. Optimal response is realized over several weeks, though long-term effects without continued use have not been proven. Take precautions to not overtighten the corset, as this can result in pain and other undesirable effects. The corset should be moderately tight and worn for only three hours per day, not during exercise or long periods of standing. Ann Chery (annchery.com) carries a variety of waist trainer corset styles and colors to choose from. Angel Curves is a waist trainer brand that Kim Kardashian has been photographed in, therefore they have renamed their product the Kardashian Waist Trainer (angelcurves.com).

Seven Weeks to Sexy – Step 5: Diet and Nutrition

You are what you eat, and your diet is important when you want to be your sexiest. In addition to adopting a healthier lifestyle related to exercise and activity, diet and nutrition are similarly important when approaching beauty from a truly holistic perspective. Some of the important supplements in the diet needed for healthy hair and skin have already been mentioned. But adopting some general practices regarding your diet and nutrition can provide that healthy glow others will immediately perceive as attractive and gorgeous.

- Reduce Carbs – If you are going to run a half marathon the next day, or if you plan on trekking up a mountain trail to the summit, then by all means, carbo-load away. But for routine activity levels, reducing carbohydrate intake is important. Stay away from processed and simple carbs (like sugars, white bread, and pasta) and lean toward foods containing whole grains and complex carbs. Too much sugar in the bodily system causes a chemical process called glycation, which has been linked to skin aging and aging of the tissues in general. Those who maintain a high sugar and carbohydrate diet form advanced glycation end products, or AGEs. Turns out, when glycation occurs and the dermal cells have AGEs attached to them, the skin is less flexible, and instead it becomes brittle and wrinkles more easily. This is the reason why diabetics age faster and have progressive organ failure much faster than the general population. Therefore, it is important not to spike your blood sugar levels by eating high carbohydrate and sugary foods—not only to lose weight but possibly to increase your longevity and improve the appearance of your skin.
- Choose Healthy Fats – Most women are aware that trans-fats and saturated fats are a no-no when trying to eat healthy and effectively manage their physique. But some fats can help promote glowing skin, silky hair, and other health benefits that boost your appearance as long as they are used in moderation.

Omega-3 and omega-6 fatty acids in fish oil are some examples of this. Likewise, polyunsaturated fats and some vegetable oils (olive oil and canola oil) have benefits that promote health and wellness. Most popular at the moment is coconut oil. Though a saturated fat, coconut oil appears to be healthy for the body because of its medium-chain fatty acids and lauric acid content; most other fats are long-chain fatty acids and contain no healing lauric acid. It can be taken as a supplemental capsule or in higher doses, up to three tablespoons a day. Kirkland Organic Virgin Pressed Coconut Oil (Costco.com) or Nature's Way Organic Extra Virgin Coconut Oil (amazon.com) taken daily offers many benefits. Coconut oil kills bacteria that cause bad breath and body odor, increases good cholesterol (HDL), and improves dry skin by increasing the oil content in your sebum. Coconut oil is anti-inflammatory and has the added benefit of adding luster to your hair.

- Eat Plenty of Proteins – Proteins (and their building blocks called amino acids) are important for healthy muscles, bones, skin, teeth, and hair. They are literally the building blocks of your body, and when in low supply, the body goes into reserve mode. Crash diets for weight loss, or strict vegan diets without plenty of protein supplement, can result in a slowdown of cell turnover. In this case, rapidly produced cells such as skin, hair, and nails are reduced to save resources for vital organs. The hair becomes thinner, skin sallower, and the nails brittle. For healthy, vibrant skin hair and nails, a high-protein diet is ideal. Lean meats are excellent sources of protein, as are some legumes, eggs, dairy, and select fruits and vegetables. These should be routinely included in your daily meals to ensure healthy tissues and to provide that healthy glow.

- Vitamins and Supplements – Consider taking vitamins and nutritional supplements to provide your body with everything it needs to be attractive and healthy. A multivitamin with iron is a given. Calcium and vitamin D are important to stave off osteoporosis. Fish oil and flax seed oil are advisable to reduce inflammation and aid in digestion. Resveratrol is a compound found in grapes that increases longevity in some animals, and thus has become a popular longevity supplement. Elysium® Basis supplements reduce NAD+ levels in our cells, presumably helping them function in a more youthful way. Glucosamine has been shown to promote hyaluronic acid synthesis in the body, thus improving skin hydration and reducing wrinkles. Heliocare® Sun Protection pills (Polypodium leucotomos) provide overall protection against photoaging by improving the body's tolerance to UV rays. Yes, an ingestible sunscreen! It only provides an SPF of 8, though, so sunscreen application is still necessary. JarroSil supplement provides bioavailable silicon. The outer cuticle of the hair shaft is rich in silicon, and therefore its availability allows hair to grow thicker and stronger. Skin and nails benefit from silicon supplementation as well. Biotin, or vitamin B7, is another effective supplement for hair, skin, and nails. Cinnamon is a powerful polyphenol antioxidant that lowers blood sugar while increasing cerebral blood flow. Turmeric (curcumin) is a dynamic antioxidant and anti-inflammatory that counters aging and age-related disease. Melatonin is a hormone produced by the pineal gland that helps regulate your circadian rhythm (day-night cycles). Taken nightly, it can aid in achieving proper amount and quality of sleep to optimize daytime energy. Of course, there are a myriad of supplements available, and new discoveries are on the horizon. Recently, collagen and antioxidant powders such as Celastin® Targeted Dermal Peptide Packets (Amazon.com) have been effective to supplement the skin's collagen. Viviscal PRO is an excellent biotin and marine extract that encourages healthy, shiny hair growth. These supplements in general should be a source of ease and provide you with a feeling of well-being.

- Avoid "AGE-ing" Foods – Do you like caramelized cheese? How about roasted coffee and crunchy bread crust? Unfortunately, these types of foods that have a burned component have been found to contain substances that accelerate the aging process of our body's cells. Advanced glycation end-products (AGEs) are specific substances in these foods that are produced when some foods are exposed to extreme heats.[89] Avoid AGEs if you are striving to look your best.

89 Claudia Luevano-Contreras and Karen Chapman-Novakofski, "Dietary advanced glycation end products and aging," *Nutrients* 2, no. 12 (2010): 1247–1265.

Seven Weeks to Sexy – Step 6: Fashion and Trends

"In fashion, only sexy won't go out of fashion." **Donatella Versace**[90]

What you wear speaks volumes about you. You may be trendy, conservative, or sexy in your daily life. Of course, you need to tailor your outfit to the occasion you are attending. What you should wear to a baby shower or a Sunday brunch is different that an evening out. Remember to unleash your sexy at the perfect time. In general, bright colors such as red, fuchsia, and melon are eye-catching and capture men's gazes for longer periods of time. In this sense, a pop of color in a conservative outfit can send a signal or a hint about your sexy side. Can solid black, white, or green also be elegant and sexy? Of course! Whatever brings out your biggest smile, best posture, and confident attitude is perfect. You have more time now to spend on your wardrobe, so you can consider some of the things we have learned in the first chapters about accentuating the waist and heel height, etc. According to Dr. Karen Pine in her book *Mind What You Wear: The Psychology of Fashion*,[91] when "we put on a piece of clothing we cannot help but adopt some of the characteristics associated with it."[92] Be a curator of your own vibe by choosing a wardrobe that says what you would like.

---

90 Daily Telegraph, "Donatella Versace says 'sexy' will never go out of fashion," 2011, retrieved from https://www.dailytelegraph.com.au/donatella-versace-says-sexy-will-never-go-out-of-fashion/news-story/c6647dba17f9ee62ade117407d3a8f8f?sv=6d048c4eb2ec784509b9322456c6f48f.
91 K. J. Pine, "Mind What You Wear: The psychology of fashion," (2014).
92 Ibid.

For Rosie Huntington-Whiteley, feeling sexy is all about Christian Louboutin heels. "They make me feel like a woman. I feel they make you look very sexy, the cuts are beautiful, the lines, the colors, the embellishments. Every girl should be lucky enough to have them." **Rosie Huntington-Whiteley**[93]

Whether you shop at a secondhand store or Barney's, you can find clothing that fits your body perfectly and instills confidence. One option is to find a stylist online or in person who will work with you. Trunkclub.com by Nordstrom offers personal wardrobe styling and free returns. This way, you can try things on with your own accessories in the comfort of your own home and keep all or none of them. Regardless of whether you use help or do it on your own, finding the right clothes should be fun and liberating. After all, we have choices and freedom to express ourselves. Let the process of discovering your look be joyful.

Seven Weeks to Sexy – Step 7: Sexuality and Sexual Health

In *Seven Days to Sexy*, we described the importance of having a positive attitude, self-confidence, and individual self-expression, and these attributes continue to play a notable role in being sexy and attractive to others. Accepting your own sexuality and embracing it underlies these attributes. During Seven Weeks to Sexy, you should consider your own sexuality and the mindset you have concerning it. Does your perspective promote greater confidence and self-esteem,

---

93 *Shape Magazine*, "What makes celebs feel sexy," n.d., retrieved from https://www.shape.com/celebrities/celebrity-photos/what-makes-celebs-feel-sexy.

or is something holding you back? Are you sabotaging yourself, and if so, why? In this case, daily affirmations are helpful. Meditation, with or without yoga, is also helpful in acceptance and discovery.

> *"I don't belong to anyone else but myself. I have to make my own decisions. Happiness is defined by me. My sexuality is defined by me. And that can change and this can change and I can make it what I want to make it because I'm the one who makes that choice. So that's what 'I Don't Belong to You,' is saying. This song feels right. It feels right and it's telling who I am. And it captures my identity."* **Keke Palmer**[94]

Sexuality is certainly a complex subject, as it describes a complicated yet essential aspect of the human experience. It affects your thoughts, fantasies, and desires, and likewise, it is an integral part of your beliefs, attitudes, values, behaviors, and relationships. How you perceive your sexuality is influenced by a variety of factors. Not only does society's perspective affect your views, but religion, spirituality, culture, and past experiences also have major impacts. How these all come together directly affects your sexual health and can also detract from or enhance how sexy and beautiful you feel. Sexiness can be mostly initiated in the mind, or it can start from visual cues or as an impulse or sensation that arises in your own body. It is so unique and individual that it behooves you to do some research about yourself.

94 Trish Bendix, "Keke Palmer and Cassie get sexy together in 'I Don't Belong to You.'" AfterEllen.com, 2015, retrieved from http://www.afterellen.com/people/459749-keke-palmer-cassie-get-sexy-together-dont-belong.

"Reading is another [thing that makes me feel sexy]. I know it sounds weird, but my definition of sexy has changed as I've gotten older. Being smart and informed makes me feel sexier than any outfit." **Sarah Shahi**[95]

So, how do you address your sexuality and your inherent reaction to it? Like most things, you first have to come to terms with who you are and what that means. Being honest with yourself about your sexual feelings and desires is very important. What piques your sexual interest? What flames your innermost desires? Answering such questions can help you dig deeper into your own unique and amazing self, and at the same time, it can help you identify areas that might be holding you back. Shame, guilt, beliefs about morality, social norms, and many other factors can come together to explain how open you are about your sexuality and how fully you express it. Of course, we are not asking you to deviate from social norms, but perhaps to open your mind to possibilities. This type of internal work takes time and self-examination.

You are who you are. Honest and open reflections about your views of sexuality and intimacy should begin with a strong dose of self-love and self-respect. This will help you release fears that hold you back from what you desire. Through these efforts, you will start the lifelong journey of allowing yourself to embrace your whole self, since sexuality cannot be truly divested from your person. The whole you will be able to enjoy a fuller life. Transmutation of sexual energy

95 Kristen Aldridge, "Up close with Sarah Shahi," *Shape Magazine*, 2012, retrieved from https://www.shape.com/celebrities/interviews/close-sarah-shahi.

can add vibrancy into every action and interaction in your day. If your sexuality is no longer suppressed, a good deal of self-control will be necessary. A type of dynamism will come over you that you perhaps have not experienced before. It will make you more attractive, more attracted, and more creative, interesting, and alive. According to Napoleon Hill, the emotion of sex contains the secret of creative ability, and some of our greatest historical minds have made use of this energy for good.[96] It behooves you to learn how to use this natural superpower that you possess.

---

96 Napoleon Hill, *Think and grow rich* (London: Hachette UK, 2011).

Chapter 6

Seven Months to Sexy

When we talked about seven days to sexy, the goal was to boost your sex appeal, confidence, and attractiveness in a short amount of time. Sometimes you have a short deadline and can do nothing about that. Then we discussed seven weeks to sexy: when you have a longer amount of time, you can choose to invest in other innovative techniques to make yourself your sexiest. Now, we come to seven months to sexy… an opportunity to not only look your absolute best but to realize your ultimate potential for beauty and confidence in every way. With this longer period of time, you have several other options to consider to help you achieve the exact look and feel you desire.

In this chapter, you will learn about some of the exciting new approaches to beauty, sexiness, and antiaging that continue to evolve in today's era of advanced science and technology. Many involve beauty-enhancing procedures that offer creative ways for you to look your best, but others provide more enduring lifestyle changes and practices that will enhance your life (and your sex appeal). As with all the beauty techniques described in this book, some will be right for you, and some will not. Regardless, simply knowing your options will allow you to select the ones that help you achieve your own specific goals, and through this, you will come to realize your most beautiful and sexiest self.

The changes that are possible in seven months are in depth, both inside and out. Consider the difference between painting your house and doing a full remodel.

Seven Months to Sexy – Step 1: Appointments and Procedures

In Seven Weeks to Sexy, we talked about several appointments and procedures you could do to enhance specific features, allowing you to look more attractive. Many of these delivered almost immediate effects in only a few sessions of care, but others required more time to realize their full beauty-enhancing effects. For example, CoolSculpting can take up to two to three months to reach its full effect, while laser hair removal and Fraxel Laser therapy typically involve a series of treatments over a few months. Naturally, the procedures and strategies discussed in Seven Weeks to Sexy will continue to be important for you in becoming your best. However, several other options become feasible when you have an even longer amount of time at your disposal. These procedures will be discussed in the following section.

In talking about various beauty-enhancing procedures, we need to clarify a couple of details up front. First, you should get all the facts about any procedure before considering if it might be right for you. While science and technology now provide us with many excellent ways to help us be sexy, each one has risks and side effects, and not every procedure is ideal for everyone. Getting the facts and knowing your own personal goals are essential when it comes to beauty-enhancing procedures. The cardinal rule of health—first do no harm! Remember that we want to look better, but radical procedures are not worth the risk and can potentially cause you to look worse, since aggressive techniques lead to an unnatural look.

The professionals you choose to advise you and to perform these procedures will be key in this regard. Choosing a board-certified plastic or oculoplastic surgeon is essential. Bargain hunting in this situation is a losing proposition. Generally, in the cosmetic world, the fees reflect what the market will bear and are indicators of how much demand for a particular surgeon exists. Reputation is everything. So, ask around and read as much as you can. Remember that even the most skilled surgeon can occasionally have a poor outcome because the human body (as well as how it heals) is variable. A healthy amount of caution is certainly logical.

Not everyone who performs these procedures has the same level of skill or style. Many of the techniques and procedures to be discussed are quite complex and require expertise and experience because they involve working with detailed anatomical structures of the face and body. Likewise, different specialists will prefer different approaches and may have a particular style when it comes to the final cosmetic result. Doing your homework about the professional who will be performing the procedure, and procuring some samples of their work, is similarly important when considering these more advanced procedures. With these caveats, we can now talk about some of the exciting beauty-enhancing options that are available today.

The American Society of Plastic Surgeons provides statistics every year on the top five cosmetic procedures. Breast augmentation, liposuction, nose reshaping, eyelid surgery, and face-lift are consistently the five most popular, and for good reason. Let's discuss a few that may potentially fulfill part of your seven-month plan.

- *Facing Change – Face-lifts* – Sagging facial tissues, deep wrinkles and creases, tired-looking eyes…these can make us feel less beautiful and confident in our appearance. Unfortunately, these features can develop over time as skin elasticity declines and the amount of tissue shrinks in volume. While many noninvasive options exist, people do reach a point where they desire a more long-term, definitive solution, and fortunately, a number of these exist. One option involves a face-lift…a plastic surgery procedure designed to tighten the skin, lift sagging tissues, and smooth deep skin folds. Face-lifts can vary from a "mini" face-lift, which typically involves very short incisions along the hairline near the ear that can be done under local anesthesia, to a full face-lift requiring more extensive facial muscle lifting and incisions along the hairline, temples, and ears. Both can correct jowling, refine the jawline, and address sagging and wrinkles, but the more invasive procedure allows greater opportunities for tissue repositioning and the creation of a firmer tissue foundation. Face-lifts are generally associated with bruising and swelling for a couple of weeks to months with a gradual return to normal activities over about a month. Also, strict avoidance of sun exposure is important, particularly during healing. The benefits can be tremendous, and the effects are long lasting.

- *An Eye for Change – Eyelid and Brow Lifts* – While face-lifts address cosmetic needs in the lower face, eyelid and brow lifts help with similar problems of the upper face. Bags under the eyes, sagging skin, eyelid puffiness, and furrowed brow lines can all be corrected and improved through various lifting techniques. For eyelids, upper or lower blepharoplasty are a possibility; these involve making tiny incisions along the edges or natural creases of the eyelids to avoid visible scarring. Excess skin and fat are then removed, and surrounding muscles are adjusted for the desired look. For brow lifts, a limited endoscopic procedure can be used to help lift tissues and remove excess fat. Or alternatively, the surgeon can make small incisions behind each temple for greater access to the tissues behind the forehead. In many cases, eyelid and brow lifts are done together, and often a face-lift is performed all at the same time. The overall recovery time is the same as for face-lifts, with bruising and swelling for a couple of weeks and a gradual return to normal activities over a month. With eyelid lifts, additional precautions must be taken to safeguard the eyes after surgery (including the use of eye lubricants, cold compresses, eye rest, and avoidance of lifting or straining during the month after surgery). Once healed, results are most often quite positive and offer a more enduring, youthful appearance.

- *Saying Yes to Nose – Rhinoplasty* – Most everyone is familiar with the nose job when it comes to plastic surgery, but the actual reasons for having rhinoplasty can be quite varied. While some may simply wish to straighten their nose or reduce its size, others may want to invest more in creating an entirely new shape. And some need these procedures to correct breathing difficulties. Because goals can differ, the type of cosmetic surgery performed with rhinoplasty can similarly vary a great deal. For example, open rhinoplasty, which involves a small incision under the tip of the nose between the nostrils, is used for more extensive reshaping. Closed rhinoplasty, on the other hand, only requires small incisions inside the nostril for more minor adjustments. And still other techniques may involve only the tip of the nose or use dermal fillers to reshape nose irregularities.
- The use of dermal fillers is one of my personal favorites. It is amazing what can be done to correct imperfections and reshape all aspects of the nose with artfully placed fillers—without the use of surgery. When surgery is selected, bruising and swelling last a couple of weeks, with a gradual return to normal activities over a month. Nasal splints are also required immediately afterward to protect the nose, and nostril packing is routinely in place for the first week. On the bright side, rhinoplasty offers lifelong changes that can make you feel more confident and attractive, so as long as expectations are realistic, rhinoplasty may be ideal for those women who prefer a different look. In Southern California, it is fairly common to have this procedure

done at sixteen years of age when a girl is becoming a young lady. Mothers, in fact, ask me on a daily basis to refer them to a plastic surgeon with a great reputation for noses.

- *Beauty Beneath the Chin – Neck Procedures* – There is no lack of names people have for the changes they see in their mirror. Turkey necks, a sagging wattle, double chin, or wrinkly neck are just a few common phrases to describe various less-than-desirable changes to the neck area. These are a telltale sign of aging, and neck procedures that eliminate these unwanted sags offer obvious ways to enhance your beauty and confidence. As with face-lifts and other "lift" procedures, neck lifts can also tighten tissues and remove excess skin and fat. After small incisions are made behind each ear and under the chin, excess skin can be removed and the underlying muscles tightened, ridding you of that extra tissue hanging from your neck. Bruising and swelling are mild, and most women can return to normal activities in a couple of weeks with a chin compression garment being required only the first three or four days after surgery. As an alternative, some women may be candidates for neck liposuction. Liposuction is ideal for younger women with good skin elasticity, since the fat removed from underneath the skin will require the skin to retract and tighten afterward to achieve a more natural and youthful look. Neck liposuction requires small incisions behind the ears and under the chin as well, but the recovery is faster and the procedure less invasive. Both neck procedures offer great long-lasting results.

Newer treatments that are nonsurgical and used to treat that double chin include CoolSculpting and Kybella® injections. CoolSculpting freezes that fat, allowing the body to clear it away over time. It requires no surgery, incisions, or down time. Kybella is an injectable agent that ruptures fat cells and similarly allows the body to clear the damaged fat away in time. These do not require incisions and have minimal down time. Last, some new endoscopic surgical techniques also exist for face and neck lifts and are offered by surgeons in larger cosmopolitan areas (neck corset/ponytail lift). Stay tuned for great innovations in both surgical and nonsurgical facial rejuvenation techniques in the near future.

- *The Top of the Hourglass – Breast Procedures* – Like rhinoplasty, women may consider breast procedures for many different reasons. For example, some women may want a larger breast size while others may want a reduction. Others are unhappy with the shape of their breast or may have experienced dramatic changes over time in breast shape due to excessive weight loss, pregnancy, and/or breastfeeding. Therefore, a variety of cosmetic procedures involving the breasts exist, and of these, breast augmentation and breast lifts are the most common.

  For breast augmentation, implants are placed to enhance breast appearance and shape, with silicone and saline implants being the most common types. A highly cohesive silicone—endearingly termed "gummi bear" fillers—also exists, allowing the breast shape to be better molded according to desired preferences. In addition to these choices, different incisional options also exist. Short incisions underneath the breast crease may be preferred, or incisions may be concealed by making surgical cuts around the areola, the armpit, or even the belly button. Depending on the extent of the surgery and the type of implant wanted, cosmetic surgeons can help guide you in determining which type of implant and surgery is ideal for you.

For women who do not want implants, breast lift procedures are also available. These "lifts" serve to reshape and recontour breasts that are asymmetric, sagging, or have fallen by removing excess or stretched-out skin while reshaping underlying breast tissues. Here again, a variety of different incisions can be considered depending on the extent of reshaping needed.

Both types of cosmetic breast procedures require a couple of weeks for bruising and swelling to resolve, but most activities can be resumed within a month. The use of a surgical bra is typically required for several weeks after the procedures, and sleeping on one's back during this time may be required.

- *The Bottom of the Hourglass – Tummy Tuck and Liposuction Procedures* – Just as cosmetic breast surgeries provide better upper-body sculpting, these procedures allow you to pursue the shape you desire when it comes to the waist, hips, and buttocks. Liposuction techniques were previously mentioned when discussing various options in neck contouring, but these same techniques are also used to reshape the belly, thighs, hips, and even chest. Liposuction removes excess fat cells from unwanted areas, and it requires a small incision where a small catheter is inserted to "suck" out the fat tissue. While this is the basic process, different liposuction techniques vary slightly. Some use ultrasound or lasers to help loosen fat cells from the underlying skin and tissues, while others inject a tumescent anesthetic solution to reduce pain and bleeding. Overall, liposuction is quite effective since it removes fat cells that will not be able to return. However, ideal candidates for the procedure need to have good skin elasticity so that skin tightens up over the areas where fat was removed, and they should also be near their ideal body weight.

Liposuction leaves only a few tiny scars, and recovery is rather quick, with most women returning to normal activities within a week or so. A tummy tuck, on the other hand, is a more advanced cosmetic procedure that seeks to flatten and firm up the stomach area. Abdominal muscles are tightened, and excess fat and skin is removed, so this offers an alternative for women who may lack adequate skin elasticity for liposuction. A tummy tuck can be limited to the area below the belly button, or it can involve the entire stomach area and even the flank area of the lower back. These procedures also tend to be more involved with a moderate amount of discomfort and a more gradual return to activities over a month or more.

- *It's All About the Bass – Buttock Procedures* – Some of the most popular trends in cosmetics today involve those that enhance the buttocks. From lifts to implants, these procedures allow you to enhance your curvaceous figure, and in some cases, remove areas where unwanted fatty tissue is hiding. For women who have good skin tone and an adequate amount of fat tissue, a butt lift may be a procedure to consider. During this procedure, excess fat is removed from the hips, abdomen, and/or thighs, and the removed fat cells are prepared and injected into the buttocks for an enhanced effect. A butt lift does require you to avoid sitting for up to eight weeks after the procedure, but the benefits can be significant and long lasting if you maintain a healthy weight.

Alternatively, for lean women who lack adequate fatty tissue, a buttock implant might be a better option. Buttock implants allow an enhanced shape and help attain an hourglass figure, but at the same time, they may feel less natural when compared to butt lifts. In addition, implants carry a greater risk for infection and scar tissue formation, so talking about the pros and cons with a qualified expert is essential when deciding about these types of procedures. Implants may look nice when standing, but they can look like upside-down Tupperware when bent over.

If implants are not a good option for you, your surgeon may suggest dermal fillers, which also can enhance buttock shape and size. This latter option is less invasive and offers a quicker recovery time when compared to other procedures that offer a shapelier hind side. Definitely, fillers are popular options for buttock and hip area enhancements that create that hourglass appearance and directly enhance the waist-to-hip ratio. Fillers should be performed by a highly skilled and experienced injector who injects either hyaluronic acid or poly-L-lactic acid in a diffuse manner. The procedure should also be done as a series and not all at once. The injections that carry the highest risk for infection are depot injections where all the material is injected as one large bolus. The filler can then point and drain, causing significant scarring and asymmetry in some cases. Patience is key. The use of temporary fillers that have good durability is ideal because this trend may not last forever. As you recall, we went through the Twiggy phase and the Farrah Fawcett buxom phase of large breast implants in the past, and now we are trending toward the booty phase as J-Lo and the Kardashians have made it more than OK to have a "big, big booty."

- *Intimate Considerations – Feminine Rejuvenation Procedures* – In addition to the more publicly discussed cosmetic surgical and nonsurgical options, feminine rejuvenation procedures are becoming a trend. For some women, such procedures provide the chance to improve vaginal tone, labial appearance, or even labial symmetry. But for others, these procedures address common issues like vaginal dryness, urinary incontinence, and even pain during intercourse. Vaginal rejuvenation procedures can be categorized as surgical and nonsurgical. In terms of surgical options, procedures include labiaplasty—removal of excess labial skin, vaginoplasty—tightening the muscles and tissue of the vaginal canal, clitoral hood reduction—removal of excess skin covering the clitoris, and mons pubis reduction or augmentation.

Some surgeons also recommend transferring fat to the inside of the vaginal walls to provide cushioning and greater fullness or sensation. These procedures remove excess skin and tissue in specific areas while tightening muscles and connective tissue at the same time. These approaches are ideal for women who desire a more permanent solution or who are considering more extensive changes. For surgical options, extensive healing time may be required and can often be anywhere from six weeks to six months. Some patients who have undergone this procedure have had pain upon intercourse in the early months after their recovery; however, with time the tissues soften and the pain typically subsides.

Regarding nonsurgical options, recent techniques involve radiofrequency energy and laser therapies. ThermiVa® is a technique that uses radiofrequency energy to heat the tissues to stimulate collagen production and subsequent tightening. MonaLisatouch® is another technique that uses a CO2 laser to stimulate cell growth, muscle strength and tone, and improved circulation. Both are noninvasive, take only minutes to perform, and require ongoing sessions for a maintained effect over months. Of these nonsurgical options, radiofrequency therapies tend to have a lowest risk of tissue scarring over time. At the moment there are at least twelve devices on the market promoting "women's health." These are changes women want but are unsure what to ask for. Likewise, these are also something laser device companies want to market but are unsure how to pitch.

There are definitely women in our practice who are suddenly single for various reasons and would love to feel more confident about their "tone." Clarifying your specific goals, both long term and short term, will allow your physician to guide you in selecting the best option to meet your needs.

Seven Months to Sexy – Step 2: Long-Term Skin and Facial Care

When it comes to long-term skin and facial care, the recommendations discussed in the "Seven Weeks to Sexy" chapter continue to provide ongoing benefits to a more youthful and attractive look as the months pass. Therefore, you will want to keep up your routine in this regard. But in addition to these healthy habits, two additional options are available, especially when it relates to facial treatments. These include a Silhouette InstaLift® and platelet-rich plasma (PRP) injections—and in the near future, stem cell therapy.

- *Silhouette InstaLift* – This office-based procedure is an alternative for women who do not wish to have a face-lift but still want to reduce facial sags and wrinkles. Overall, the entire treatment takes about forty-five minutes and consists of having tiny biodegradable suture "cones" placed along the cheek and jawline. These cones are composed of the same material from which absorbable sutures are made, and once placed, they gradually dissolve and are absorbed by the body. When absorbed, the suture cord is replaced by your own collagen. The material of which this suture is made stimulates collagen production.

Once the suture is resorbed, the skin remains lifted where the sutures used to be while collagen is stimulated in the area, allowing tissues to have more volume. The current sutures used are an improvement on the permanent Prolene sutures used in the past. Because of this, the procedure can be repeated when necessary with no residual material left in the skin. For women who may not be ready for a face-lift, this is a great option, as its effects last eighteen months.

- *PRP Injections* – Platelet-rich plasma is your own blood serum with a concentrated buffy coat—which includes your platelets—resuspended into the serum. Platelets contain alpha granules that degranulate or open up at the site of an injury. When the body detects an injury, it sends out eight different growth factors that provide messages to your body that tissue healing is required and the laying down of new collagen is necessary. You may wonder why this does not occur continually since you have platelets coursing through your veins at all times. The difference is that platelets are only outside the blood vessel when tissue injuries occur, and once they are outside, they provide granules that release growth factors including VEGF (vascular endothelial growth factor), PDGF (platelet derived growth factor), EGF (epidermal growth factor), insulin-like growth factor, TGF beta (transforming growth factor), and more. These growth factors and other components trigger tissue growth and rejuvenation. By injecting your own PRP into facial skin through microneedling procedures, as well as to the underside of the skin via traditional injections (in the dermis, where your collagen lives), rejuvenation can be stimulated. PRP can be used to reduce wrinkles, stimulate collagen, and create a more youthful skin appearance using your own natural growth factors. PRP is harvested from your own blood, usually through a simple blood draw, and then the material is centrifuged. The serum and platelet portion is then introduced into the skin over the course of three to six treatments for the desired effect. Microneedling with "smearing" of the PRP into the skin is a popular procedure that augments the injection of PRP into the skin. The treatment can be combined with Fraxel resurfacing or other laser treatments to augment healing. Results appear as early as a few days later and improve over the following months. A series of three to six monthly treatments is recommended.

- *Stem Cell Therapy* – Stem cells are fascinating and have been studied for many years in the pursuit for disease cures. Stems cells are the human body's master cells. They have the ability to grow into any one of the body's more than two-hundred-plus cell types. As unspecialized cells, stem cells contain the same genetic background information, and they retain the ability to divide throughout life that can ultimately give rise to highly specialized cells that can take the place of cells that die or are lost. Stem cells thus contribute significantly to the body's ability to renew and repair its tissues. Unlike mature cells that are permanently committed to their fate, stem cells can renew themselves and create new cells of a number of different tissue types. Bone marrow stem cells are the most primitive stem cells from which all cells are descended. This explains why bone marrow transplants are used to treat some cell disorders. There is one caveat, however. The DNA of these transplanted cells must significantly match the cells of the recipient in order for them to "take." DNA must be compatible. In fact, the perfect match for a stem cell is your own.

Believe it or not, stem cells are also stored in your own fat (adipose tissue). That fatty tissue we have all been trying to lose might actually become our new treasure trove. During the aging process, the number of stem cells present throughout the body gradually decreases. Because of this, cells begin to die faster and do not have the same quality that they once had. Declining levels of adult stem cells mean that cellular damage can be essentially left unrepaired almost anywhere in the body. The older we get, the more our body must redirect resources to vital organs and away from hair, skin, and nails. However, stem cell treatments can restore and replenish tissues in key areas of concern. They must not only be "moved" to the desired location, but they must be activated at the same time. Based on the cells nearby, stem cells know which type of cell they need to replenish. This is known as cellular induction. But again, the transferred cells must be activated as well, and overall, stem cell activity declines with age despite their preserved potential. New techniques (like parabiosis where stem cells are bathed in younger cells and telomere extension methods) are currently being tested to activate stem cells, but these methods are still being perfected.

Needless to say, stem cells are quite tricky and complex. Stem cell therapy has the potential promise of restoring health and youth, but it must be done correctly. Stem cell creams that are available today seem unlikely to be able to stimulate regeneration in the same ways that genetically identical living stem cells could. However, ethical issues exist regarding stem cell activation; therefore, regulations are in place. Regardless, this burgeoning therapy is moving forward like a freight train, so it is only a matter of time before these pluripotent stem cells are harnessed to introduce a revolutionary new era in health and beauty. You might just be standing on the edge of your very own fountain of youth!

Seven Months to Sexy – Step 3: Advanced Hair Considerations

As with skin and facial care, continued commitment to performing daily and weekly hair care regimens will allow progressive results in the look and feel of your hair. But what happens if hair loss or even bald patches begin to be a problem? In addition to proper hair care and nutrition, some additional options exist for hair care that are worth noting when trying to look your best over the long term.

- *Minoxidil* – This medication was originally used to treat high blood pressure, but it was then noted to have a side effect of promoting hair growth. Minoxidil usually comes as a topical

2 or 5% solution, commonly known as Rogaine®, that can be applied once or twice a day. The medication blocks specific types of testosterone receptors and therefore modifies testosterone's effect on the scalp follicles. Testosterone interestingly causes body hair to grow and scalp hair to thin after a certain age.

- *Finasteride* – Known under the trade name of Propecia®, this medication allows some hair growth and mostly works by preventing further hair loss. The medication lowers response to a form of testosterone (dihydrotestosterone), which results in the desired effects. This medication is often combined with minoxidil in men to reduce male pattern baldness, but it similarly can be safely used for women as well.
- *PRP Creams and Injections* – Previously, PRP was discussed for facial rejuvenation with or without microneedling, but did you know it is also used for hair growth stimulation? Because PRP contains concentrated growth factors and other cell stimulating substances, it has been shown to help stimulate hair growth and prevent hair loss. PRP creams can be applied to the scalp or other areas where hair growth normally occurs with some notable benefits being reported. PRP creams are created using your own platelet-rich plasma.

Seven Months to Sexy – Step 4: Refined Body Sculpting through Exercise

> *Running a marathon made Alison Sweeney really believe in herself, and that equals sexy. "I totally hit the runner's wall at mile 21 and it was easily the hardest thing I've ever done to keep going. Fitness helps you get in touch with who you are."* **Alison Sweeney**[97]

When considering exercise and body sculpting over many months, you will naturally see progressive results the more consistently you are in performing your routine. While rapid weight loss and increases in muscle tone may occur in days to weeks with a good exercise regimen, the real benefit comes after many months of dedicated commitment. The key is to not give up. With that in mind, here are some tips to help you stay focused on your long-term goal of being your sexiest through healthy, fun exercise.

- *Mix It Up* – The greatest obstacle to a person's commitment to a regular exercise routine is simply boredom. Who wants to get on a treadmill every day of their life, or even do the same "body pump" routine again? We are not robots, and we need variety to stimulate our interest and excitement. Therefore, be sure to have several different exercise activities and routines from which to choose from.

---

97 *Shape Magazine*, "What makes celebs feel sexy," n.d., retrieved from https://www.shape.com/celebrities/celebrity-photos/what-makes-celebs-feel-sexy.

- *Choose Fun Activities* – Just as we need variety, we also need to have fun. If your exercise is fun, then you don't have to overcome many of the barriers that keep you from exercising on a regular basis. So many options to be active exist, so simply survey your options and select those that you are certain to enjoy. Get creative! Hiking, ballroom dancing, pole dancing and wall climbing are a few fun and exciting activities that come to mind.
- *Be Social* – Going it alone can be challenging, even when exercise might be somewhat fun and varied. Participating in group activities adds a social dimension that can also help you stay on track. For some women, having a personal trainer also serves this role. In addition to providing an opportunity to meet and share with others, you also benefit from an accountability factor since others may notice your absence.
- *Create Goals* – Nothing helps keep you motivated like a specific goal you want to achieve. Perhaps your goal is a specific weight you want to achieve. Maybe you want to get your waist or hips a certain size. Regardless of your own personal desires, set a goal or goals to help you stay focused and motivated as you commit to your regular exercise routine. Writing down your short, midrange, and long-term goals is a helpful exercise in helping you get yourself from where you are currently to where you would like to be.

Seven Months to Sexy – Step 5: Nutritional and Hormonal Options

Like exercise, attention to healthy nutrition continues to provide positive results over time. The more you stay hydrated, eat fruits and vegetables, and avoid foods associated with an accelerated aging process, the more vibrant and radiant you will look and feel. In addition to the previously mentioned nutritional strategies for enhanced wellness and beauty, other therapies are also receiving a great deal of attention as well. These include various hormonal therapies with touted antiaging effects that may preserve youthfulness. However, use of these substances needs to be individualized, and you also should have a good understanding of potential side effects. Here are a few of the more common hormonal therapies offered today.

- *DHEA* – This hormone is a precursor to other hormones in the body like estrogen, progesterone, and testosterone. It has been used to enhance energy levels, improve muscle strength, build a strong immune system, and promote leaner body mass in specific cases. Overall, these features are believed to slow the aging process and enhance youthfulness, as well as libido, particularly in women, but the effects vary. DHEA can be taken as a daily oral supplement.
- *Human Growth Hormone hGH* – Human growth hormone is a small protein made by the pituitary gland. The levels vary during the day and night, so it is tricky to get a handle on one's hGH level. hGH supplementation has been used extensively to

help reduce some of the effects of aging. Specifically, it has been associated with increased muscle mass, reduced amounts of body fat, and even enhanced libido. This hormone is certainly not for everyone, and make sure you are monitored for side effects.

- *Melatonin* – This hormone is naturally produced by a tiny gland in the brain known as the pineal gland, and it is best known for keeping our sleep schedule on track. We all need our beauty sleep! But at the same time, melatonin may offer some other antiaging effects related to its anti-inflammatory properties. Three to nine milligrams every night at the same time helps to regulate sleep-wake cycles. Sleep-wake cycles are important for cognition, memory, weight control, focus, and a sense of well-being. New studies are underway regarding melatonin's antiaging effects as well since the aging brain reportedly shows a decline in natural melatonin production over time.
- *Estrogen and Progesterone* – Most women are familiar with these hormones, especially once perimenopausal symptoms appear. The use of these hormones around menopause can help reduce unwanted symptoms like hot flashes and improve conditions like vaginal dryness. Estrogen supports collagen production and promotes a youthful appearance of the skin. In contrast, withdrawal of estrogen causes sallow skin with the appearance of deeper lines. Other antiaging effects may be present as well, but the pros and cons of taking these hormones long term must be weighed before choosing to add these to your regimen. A family or personal history of clotting disorder and/or

estrogen positive breast cancer are examples of contraindications for hormone replacement. With proper history, physical exam, pelvic ultrasound, and blood monitoring, hormone replacement may be an option. If so, it can significantly improve one's quality of life.

Seven Months to Sexy – Step 6: Organic Evolution of Fashion and Wardrobe

> *"Sexy is about the way you wear something and being confident; the clothes are sexy and flattering. I've said right from the beginning, it's very important clothes are flattering. I want a woman to look and feel like the best version of herself."* **Victoria Beckham**[98]

If you periodically look back over old photographs of yourself, you appreciate how your style in fashion changes over time. In part, this is due to changes in society, but other factors also play a role including your stage in life, your age, your attitude, and others. Once you have committed to being your most sexy self by applying some of the strategies proposed in this book, you will likely find your taste in fashion and clothing will change once again. As your confidence begins to soar, and as your shape and figure begin to change, so will your choices in what you wear.

98 Emma Spedding, "'I do like to make things difficult for myself': Victoria Beckham on her SS17 collection, her family life and always being camera ready," *Telegraph*, 2016, retrieved from https://www.telegraph.co.uk/fashion/new-york-fashion-week/victoria-beckham-spring-summer-2017-new-york-fashion-week-show-h/.

In "Seven Months to Sexy," you should be aware of these changes and allow your choice in fashion to evolve organically. Perhaps you begin admiring a specific style you would have never considered before. Or maybe you simply feel the need for an entire clothing makeover to fit with the new you. Go with these impulses. They are not accidental. The important thing is to recognize this as being a part of the ongoing journey on which you have embarked to become more beautiful and sexy. When these urges surface, don't suppress them. Simply let them express the new you so you can realize your complete potential. Being a little daring is all right on occasion. If your new clothing preferences don't go over well, then look at it as a learning experience. The idea is to click into your style and feel perfectly comfortable in your clothing.

Seven Months to Sexy – Step 7: Exploring Sexuality and Enlightenment

> *"I feel much better about myself, actually. When you get older you start to have respect for yourself and value certain things and choices you've made in your life that have given you strength. I'm much more comfortable with who I am, and I'm even thinking that I don't look so bad. I feel a lot sexier these days than I ever have."* **Reese Witherspoon**[99]

Last, we come to the spiritual side of sexuality and sexiness. Our desire for sexual expression is innate and natural, and these desires should

99 *Shape Magazine*, "What makes celebs feel sexy," n.d., retrieved from https://www.shape.com/celebrities/celebrity-photos/what-makes-celebs-feel-sexy.

not be suppressed or ignored. Oftentimes, we may have experienced things in our past that stop us from pursuing activities and choices that help us fulfill these desires. In "Seven Months to Sexy," we have suggested that you explore specific barriers and obstacles that prevent you from achieving more complete self-expression. What holds you back? What limits you? Find you specific individual barriers and make a commitment to overcome them in a constructive, healthy way.

> *"Sexuality will always be a part of how I express myself artistically. I don't think a woman should be afraid of her sexuality."* **Christina Aguilera**[100]

From this perspective, you may choose to approach your sexuality and spirituality in a variety of ways. Some choose to find a life coach to help them unlock their personal power and potential. Others prefer meditation and self-examination in a secluded manner. Regardless of the approach you choose, seek to find outlets in your body, mind, and spirit where sexual expression can happen. As highlighted in the teachings of Napoleon Hill, sexual energies can be transmuted or transformed into other energies that enable success in all areas of your life.[101] Embracing your sexuality and seeking these opportunities can help you become the person you were intended to be, and that will always be the "you" who is the most beautiful and sexy.

---

100 *Cosmopolitan Magazine*, "The hot things celebs tell Cosmo," 2011, retrieved from https://www.cosmopolitan.com/entertainment/celebs/news/g1326/sexy-quotes-from-cosmo-cover-girls/.
101 D. P. Kimbro, D. Kimbro, & N. Hill, *Think and grow rich: A Black choice* (New York: Fawcett, 1992).

Conclusion

Years ago, a couple was looking to purchase their first home. Having just moved into the area, they had to make a decision fast. The wife was starting a new job the following month, and she wanted to get settled as soon as possible. Likewise, the husband had relocated to be the new social director for a local company, which meant he would likely be entertaining a lot at home. Unfortunately, they not only had limited time but also a limited budget. After visiting home after home, nothing seemed to have that instant sex appeal they wanted. So, they decided to get a fixer-upper that had some inherent charm but was in need of some significant TLC. Twenty years later, they still live in the same house, but you would never know it by driving by it today. After a series of makeovers to both the inside and out, the house is truly immaculate in every way.

When you think about being your sexiest and most attractive, many comparisons can be made between how you look, feel, and act and the original house this couple purchased years ago. Each of us has the potential to be sexy and beautiful, but from the outside, it may not be readily apparent. Even on the inside, we may not feel sexy. In order to change the way we look and feel, we have to commit to some changes. And depending on the time available, we can pursue different approaches to yield remarkable results. In essence, this book serves as a practical guide to help you do just that. Whether you have seven days, seven weeks, or seven months, you can pick and choose which activities and changes to embrace in your own personal journey toward beauty and sexiness.

From reading each of the sections, you can now appreciate that a specific, universal definition of sexiness does not exist. Each of us is an individual with our own unique features, and expressing those features fully is what truly makes one beautiful inside and out. But at the same time, some general rules apply. Behavioral psychology has taught us that specific attributes that showcase youth, energy, and vitality are often viewed as sexy and attractive, and likewise, specific behaviors and attitudes are often interpreted the same. By applying this information to your own unique self, you can ultimately embrace your own version of sexiness that feels right for you. And in the process, you can enjoy a heightened level of confidence and satisfaction never before realized. That is what being beautiful is all about.

Naturally, not every activity and suggestion made in the previous chapters applies to everyone, and choosing those which best help you achieve your own goals is important. This requires you to take an inventory of how you look, how you feel, how you behave, and your own personal mindset so that you can best determine where to start. Even if you have a week to become your best, several strategies can help you look and feel beautiful in no time. And with longer periods of time, your opportunities expand tremendously. With a good understanding of what is beautiful and sexy for you, you can pick specific tasks to prepare you for any event no matter when it is. Thus, the suggestions made in this book can serve as a practical guide of recipes and schedules to best meet your needs. Soon, these choices can become second nature, and instead of doing a mad scramble to look your best, you will ease into the seven weeks and then seven months version of being your best at all times as a lifestyle.

It should be noted that the techniques to enhance beauty described reflect those that are available today, but certainly new and exciting developments are ongoing. New products and procedures come to market rapidly, as this is an ever-evolving, well-funded field. Besides devices, products, and procedures, advances in the stem cell arena are moving at an accelerated pace. Instead of pursuing procedures to correct signs of aging as they occur, we may be able to address aging in advance. In the years to come, these technologies and others will likely offer additional opportunities for enhancing beauty. Regardless, understanding current procedures and approaches to enhance beauty will provide you a solid foundation upon which to consider new ones in the future. Therefore, *Seven Days to Sexy* can continue to be a valuable resource for you both now and over time.

Let's face it. Each of us wants to be sexy, beautiful, and attractive. As individuals, we have an innate need to express ourselves in this way, and being able to do so allows us to be our best selves. The way we look affects how we feel inside and how we behave, and likewise, how we act and think influence the level of commitment we make in looking our most beautiful. Sexiness is a holistic concept that involves mind, body, and spirit, and by accepting this perspective of personal beauty, you will begin to realize opportunities and excitement you never imagined possible. So, what are you waiting for? It's time for you to pull out all the stops and be the absolute sexiest you can be!

ABOUT THE AUTHOR

Anna Guanche, MD, FAAD, is a board-certified dermatologist, celebrity beauty expert, and founder of Bella Skin Institute located in Calabasas, California. Affectionately known as "Dr. Beauty," Dr. Guanche specializes in cosmetic dermatology, antiaging, and beauty enhancements utilizing state-of-the-art skin rejuvenation procedures, laser surgery, and injectables. In addition to her private practice, which is one of only two private clinic sites approved to teach UCLA dermatology residents, Dr. Guanche was a member of the dermatology staff at UCLA Olive View Medical Center, where she taught for 13 years.

A sought-after lecturer, Dr. Guanche has been voted Los Angeles Magazine's "Super Doctor" by her peers for seven consecutive years.

Understanding that there is a constant need for learning and growth in the field, Dr. Guanche never sits still; instead, she constantly strives to be ahead of the curve in her specialty and has been called "The Steve Jobs of Dermatologists" for her innovation. Her desire to deliver more led to the development of the GuancheLift, BellaFX, and her own unique concoction with Aquagold to give patients a real-life airbrushed look. With a deep passion for helping people feel better, both medically and cosmetically, Dr. Guanche takes an artistic approach to cosmetic dermatology and truly adores connecting with her patients.

Staff and patients alike connect to Dr. Guanche's charismatic, silly, and fun personality. Her patients love being around her and often leave the office feeling like they have just seen a close friend. Dr. Guanche's clientele includes everyone from teens and retirees, CEOs, supermoms, and celebrities such as Alyssa Milano, Terry Ellis, Rebecca Romijn, Eva LaRue, Miss Universe 2012 Olivia Culpo, singer/songwriter Natalie Imbruglia, Jerry O'Connell, McKenzie Westmore, Real Housewives of Beverly Hills actress Brandi Glanville, Brittany Furlan, as well as other A-list film and television stars seen on the red carpet.

She knows, however, that even the most famous women need a serious bit of preparation in order to walk the red carpet or perform a television interview. In fact, many of Dr. Guanche's patients are the celebrity stylists, makeup artists, and hairdressers who make the magic happen. Having been a visitor on the red carpet numerous times herself, Dr. Guanche has learned the behind the scenes secrets of looking epic for an event, from posture and medical procedures to outfits and makeup and hair.

Dr. Guanche's expertise has been featured on Extra, Entertainment Tonight, KTLA, MSN, in ELLE, Glamour, Prevention, Shape, SELF, InStyle, Health, Yahoo!, HuffPost, Bustle, Byrdie, and PopSugar, as well as on the Emmy-winning daytime show The Doctors, just to name a few!

Dr. Anna Guanche is a Fellow of the American Board of Dermatology, and a member of the American Academy of Dermatology,